Good Housekeeping

Best Pasta Dishes
& Sauces

Good Housekeeping

Best Pasta Dishes
& Sauces

LIMITED EDITIONS
BOOKTITLES

This edition published for Limited Editions in 1996
First published in 1995 by Ebury Press
an imprint of Random House UK Ltd
Random House
20 Vauxhall Bridge Road
London SW1V 2SA

Random House Australia (Pty) Limited
20 Alfred Street, Milsons Point, Sydney
New South Wales 2061, Australia

Random House New Zealand Limited
18 Poland Road, Glenfield
Auckland 10, New Zealand

Random House South Africa (Pty) Limited
PO Box 337, Bergvlei, South Africa

Random House UK Limited Reg. No. 954009

A CIP catalogue record for this book is available from the British Library.

ISBN: 0 09 180737 9

Editor: Helen Southall
Design: Christine Wood
Photography by: Laurie Evans and Graham Kirk

Front cover photo (Graham Kirk): Walnut and Bacon Sauce, page 74.
Back cover photo (Graham Kirk): Creamy Pasta Bake, page 103.

Printed and bound in Singapore

CONTENTS

INTRODUCTION

The word pasta simply means 'dough' in Italian but it is also used to describe spaghetti, macaroni, lasagne and many other pasta shapes made from the basic dough mixture. There are said to be over 500 different varieties of pasta throughout Italy today, although only about 50 of these are widely known. The best commercially dried pasta is made from 100 per cent hard durum wheat; look for this description, or *pasta di semola di grano duro*, on the packet. There is a vast selection of dried pasta shapes to choose from. Most dried pastas are made from durum wheat and water, but some are made from *pasta all'uovo* (egg pasta).

Fresh pasta is made from flour and eggs, and is becoming increasingly easy to buy. Most supermarkets stock a good range, and Italian delicatessens invariably make their own. However, nothing can compare with the flavour and freshness of home-made pasta (see page 8).

As for nutritional value, pasta is mainly a carbohydrate food, although good-quality brands can contain as much as 13 per cent protein, and all contain some vitamins and minerals.

DIFFERENT TYPES OF PASTA
There is an increasingly wide choice of flavoured fresh and dried pasta available. Coloured pasta adds interest to meals: green pasta (*pasta verde*) is flavoured with spinach; pink or red pasta (*pasta rosso*) with tomatoes or peppers; black pasta with squid ink. Fresh pasta is also available flavoured with basil or garlic. Wholewheat pasta is available too; it contains more fibre than pasta made with ordinary flour and is consequently darker and more chewy.

The variety of pasta shapes is endless and new shapes are constantly being introduced. Here is a guide to the most common ones, although you may see slightly different shapes or the same shape under different names – especially if visiting Italy. This is simply because the different regions of Italy have their own individual pasta shapes and names – and so do the manufacturers.
SPAGHETTI comes in long straight strands of varying thickness. When cooking long dried spaghetti, coil it gently into the pan as it softens on contact with the boiling water.
MACARONI is a thicker hollow tube, sometimes cut into short lengths; *bucatini*, *tubetti*, *zite* and *penne* are all short macaroni.
LASAGNE is the widest of the ribbon pastas. It comes in flat strips, rectangles or squares with either a smooth or ridged edge. Some varieties do not need pre-cooking before using in a dish to be

baked. Both white and green varieties of lasagne (lasagne verde) are readily available.

NOODLES are narrow flat pasta strips. They are either straight ribbons or folded into a nest-shaped mass, which is easier to drop into boiling water. *Tagliatelle* and *fettucine* are the most common types.

VERMICELLI is the finest ribbon pasta. It comes in a nest-shaped mass and is mostly used in soups.

CANNELLONI are large hollow tubes which can be stuffed with meat or vegetable mixtures and served with sauce. *Rigatoni* are slightly narrower than cannelloni.

SMALL PASTA SHAPES include *lumache* (snails), *conchiglie* (shells), *fusilli* (twists), *ruotini* (wheels), *farfalle* (bows), and *cappalletti* (hats) and *orecchiette* (ears).

TINY PASTA SHAPES for use in soup include *ditalini* and *orzo* (shaped like rice grains).

STUFFED PASTA SHAPES include *ravioli*, *tortellini* and *tortelli*.

STORING PASTA

Fresh pasta should be kept in the refrigerator and used within 24 hours of purchase; after this time it begins to dry out. Unopened packets of dried pasta will keep for months in a cool, dry cupboard, but once opened, the packet should be used up quickly as exposure to the air makes the pasta brittle and tasteless.

QUANTITIES OF PASTA

When calculating how much to serve, you will need to consider appetite and how substantial the other courses are. As a rough guide, when serving as a main course dish, allow 125–150 g (4–5 oz) uncooked fresh pasta per person, or 75–125 g (3–4 oz) dried. If serving as a starter, allow 75–125 g (3–4 oz) fresh pasta per person, 50–75 g (2–3 oz) dried.

MAKING YOUR OWN PASTA

Making pasta at home is very easy – the actual dough is a simple mixture of flour, salt, eggs and olive oil. The best flour to use is semolina flour: a hard, very fine wheat flour. As this is difficult to obtain, a strong flour of the type used for making bread is a satisfactory alternative.

It is well worth investing in a pasta machine if you regularly make your own pasta. One of these can cut larger quantities more evenly and quickly than you can by hand. It will also cut various shapes.

COOKING PASTA

Pasta should be cooked in fast-boiling salted water in a large saucepan. Allow about 2–3 litres (3½–5¼ pints) per 450 g (1 lb) of pasta. Adding 15 ml (1 tbsp) oil to the water will help to prevent the pasta sticking together.

Cooking time depends on the size; long pasta takes about 8–10 minutes, short cut pasta 6–12 minutes and tiny pasta shapes 2–6 minutes. Lasagne takes about 12 minutes. Fresh pasta takes about 2–4 minutes. Brands do vary enormously, so check packet instructions. Check just before the end of the cooking time by biting a piece of pasta. It should be what the Italians call *al'dente*, firm but not too hard or soft. Once it has reached this stage it should be drained thoroughly and served immediately. If the pasta is to be used in a cold dish, rinse under cold running water and drain well. Hot pasta is always best eaten immediately, although it can be kept hot in a colander over a pan of boiling water for a few minutes.

HOME-MADE PASTA DOUGH

MAKES ABOUT 350 G (12 OZ) DOUGH

about 200 g (7 oz) semolina flour or strong white
flour
2 eggs
pinch of salt
15 ml (1 tbsp) olive oil

1 Sift the flour into a mound on a clean work surface. With your fist, make a well in the centre and add the eggs, salt and oil.
2 Using your fingertips, gradually draw in the flour into the eggs. Continue until the dough comes together.
3 Then, using both hands, knead the dough on a lightly floured surface for about 10 minutes or until smooth and not sticky.
4 Form the dough into a ball, place in a polythene bag and leave to rest for 30 minutes before shaping as required.

VARIATIONS

PASTA VERDE (SPINACH PASTA)

Wash, drain and discard the coarse stalks from 225 g (8 oz) fresh spinach. Cook in a saucepan, with no additional water, for about 5 minutes or until tender. Cool, then squeeze out all excess moisture with your hands. Finely chop. Increase the flour in the dough to 225 g (8 oz) and add the spinach with the eggs.

RED PASTA

Skin 1 medium red pepper (see page 40), then purée in a blender or food processor. Add to the flour with the eggs and oil, increasing the flour to 225 g (8 oz).

HERB PASTA

Add 30 ml (2 level tbsp) chopped fresh herbs, such as basil or parsley, to the flour with the eggs, salt and oil.

SHAPING DOUGH

If using a pasta machine, put your dough through on the chosen setting, sprinkling very lightly with flour if it is becoming sticky.

Alternatively, roll out the pasta on a floured work surface to a large rectangle which is nearly paper thin. If you are making cut pasta, such as tagliatelle, fettucine or lasagne, the dough must be allowed to dry. Place the dough on a clean tea towel, allowing one third to hang over the edge of a table or work surface, and turn every 10 minutes. The pasta is ready to cut when it is dry to the touch, after about 30 minutes.
TAGLIATELLE Lightly fold the dough over into a roll about 7.5 cm (3 inches) in depth. With a sharp knife, cut into 1 cm ($\frac{1}{2}$ inch) wide strips; try to cut them all the same width. Unfold and leave to dry for about 10 minutes.
FETTUCINE Proceed as for tagliatelle but cut the dough into 5 mm ($\frac{1}{4}$ inch) wide strips. Unfold and leave to dry.
LASAGNE Cut the dough into 10 x 15 cm (4 x 6 inch) rectangles.

SOUPS AND STARTERS

VEGETABLE AND PASTA SOUP

SERVES 4

175 g (6 oz) French beans, topped and tailed
15 ml (1 tbsp) olive oil
1 red onion, skinned and thinly sliced
2 carrots, peeled and thinly sliced
1 garlic clove, skinned and crushed
5 ml (1 level tsp) dried oregano
15 ml (1 level tbsp) tomato purée
125 g (4 oz) tomatoes, skinned, deseeded and chopped
1.4 litres (2½ pints) chicken stock
1 green chilli, deseeded and finely chopped
50 g (2 oz) dried pasta shapes
30 ml (2 level tbsp) chopped fresh coriander
30 ml (2 level tbsp) chopped fresh parsley
salt and pepper

1 Cut the French beans in half.
2 Heat the oil in a large saucepan. Add the onion, carrots, garlic and oregano, and sauté for 2-3 minutes.
3 Add the tomato purée, French beans, tomatoes and chicken stock. Bring to the boil, then reduce the heat, cover and simmer gently for about 35 minutes or until the vegetables are just tender.
4 Stir the chilli into the soup with the pasta, coriander and parsley.
5 Simmer for 10–15 minutes or until the pasta is cooked. Add salt and pepper to taste, and serve.

SUITABLE FOR FREEZING

155 Calories per serving

Overleaf: Minestrone (page12)

Minestrone

SERVES 6–8

175 g (6 oz) dried cannellini beans, soaked
overnight in cold water

60 ml (4 tbsp) olive oil

2 onions, skinned and chopped

3 garlic cloves, skinned and crushed

2 carrots, peeled and diced

2 celery sticks, trimmed and diced

400 g (14 oz) can of chopped tomatoes

2.3 litres (4 pints) vegetable stock

350 g (12 oz) floury potatoes, such as King
Edward or Maris Piper, peeled and diced

125 g (4 oz) small dried pasta shapes

125 g (4 oz) shelled fresh or frozen peas

175 g (6 oz) French beans, topped, tailed
and sliced

225 g (8 oz) dark green cabbage, tough stalks
removed and roughly chopped

75 ml (5 level tbsp) chopped fresh parsley

60 ml (4 tbsp) pesto sauce

salt and pepper

extra pesto and freshly grated Parmesan cheese,
to serve

1 Drain the beans, put them in a very large
saucepan and cover with fresh water. Bring to the
boil and boil rapidly for 10 minutes, then reduce
the heat, cover and simmer for 1 hour.

2 Meanwhile, heat the oil in a large saucepan,
add the onions and garlic, and fry for 5–10 minutes or until golden. Add the carrots and celery,
and fry for 2 minutes, stirring occasionally.

3 Drain the beans and add them to the pan with
the tomatoes, stock, potatoes, pasta and fresh
peas, if using. Stir well and bring to the boil, then
reduce the heat, half-cover and simmer for 1
hour.

4 Stir in the frozen peas, if using, French beans,
cabbage, parsley and pesto sauce. Season with salt
and pepper and simmer for 30 minutes or until
the vegetables are tender.

5 Serve immediately in a warmed soup tureen,

with the extra pesto and cheese in separate bowls
for guests to stir into their soup.

COOK'S TIP

This traditional Italian soup is hearty enough to
be a main course, simply served with chunks of
Italian bread.

SUITABLE FOR FREEZING

375–280 Calories per serving

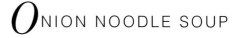

Onion Noodle Soup

SERVES 4

30 ml (2 tbsp) olive oil

550 g (1¼ lb) onions, skinned, quartered and
sliced

1 garlic clove, skinned and crushed

125 g (4 oz) thin pasta noodles, such as tagliolini
or vermicelli

1.1 litres (2 pints) vegetable stock

5 ml (1 level tsp) plain flour

1 bunch of watercress, roughly chopped

grated rind and juice of 1 lemon

salt and pepper

50 g (2 oz) Emmental cheese, grated, to serve

1 Heat the olive oil in a large, non-stick
saucepan, add the onions and garlic, cover and
cook over a very low heat for 20–30 minutes or
until the onions are softened and well browned.

2 Meanwhile, cook the pasta in the vegetable
stock for about 10 minutes, then drain, reserving
the stock.

3 Uncover the onions, increase the heat, add the
flour and cook for 1 minute. Stir in the reserved
vegetable stock and bring to the boil, then reduce
the heat and simmer for 5–7 minutes.

4 Stir the watercress into the soup with the

lemon rind and 15 ml (1 tbsp) lemon juice. Season well with salt and pepper.

5 Divide the pasta between four hot bowls and spoon the soup over it. Serve piping hot with grated Emmental cheese.

COOK'S TIP

Make sure the onions are well browned at the end of step 1, as this is what gives the soup its wonderful rich brown colour and strong, oniony flavour.

265 Calories per serving

NOT SUITABLE FOR FREEZING

CHICKEN AND PASTA BROTH

SERVES 6

two 275 g (10 oz) chicken portions, skin removed
1–2 small leeks, trimmed, sliced and washed
2 carrots, peeled and thinly sliced
900 ml (1½ pints) chicken stock
900 ml (1½ pints) water
1 bouquet garni
salt and pepper
50 g (2 oz) small dried pasta shapes
chopped fresh parsley, to garnish

1 Put the chicken portions in a large saucepan with the sliced leeks and carrots. Pour in the chicken stock and water, and bring to the boil.

2 Add the bouquet garni and salt and pepper to taste, then lower the heat, cover the pan and simmer for 30 minutes or until the chicken is tender.

3 Remove the chicken from the liquid using a slotted spoon. Set the chicken aside and leave until cool enough to handle.

4 Meanwhile, place the pasta in the pan of liquid and return to the boil. Cook for 10–12 minutes or until the pasta is just tender, stirring occasionally.

5 Remove the chicken flesh from the bones and cut the flesh into bite-sized pieces.

6 Return the chicken to the pan and heat through. Discard the bouquet garni and taste and adjust the seasoning. Serve hot in warmed soup bowls, each portion sprinkled with a little chopped parsley.

460 Calories per serving

NOT SUITABLE FOR FREEZING

SPAGHETTI WITH BUTTER AND PARMESAN

SERVES 4

225–350 g (8–12 oz) dried spaghetti
salt
50 g (2 oz) butter or margarine
50 g (2 oz) Parmesan cheese, freshly grated

1 Cook the spaghetti in boiling salted water for 10–12 minutes or until just tender.

2 Drain well and return to the pan. Add the butter or margarine and 15 g ($^1/_2$ oz) Parmesan cheese. Stir and leave for a few minutes for the butter and cheese to melt. Serve with the remaining cheese in a separate dish.

VARIATION

Add lightly cooked vegetables, such as broccoli or asparagus.

450 Calories per serving

NOT SUITABLE FOR FREEZING

SMOKED PLATTER WITH WARM PASTA SALAD

SERVES 6

350 g (12 oz) dried spaghettini (thin spaghetti)

salt and pepper

175 g (6 oz) sun-dried tomatoes in oil (you'll need a 280 g/10 oz jar), drained and roughly chopped

120 ml (8 tbsp) olive oil, preferably from the jar of sun-dried tomatoes

90 ml (6 level tbsp) chopped fresh chives or spring onions

175 g (6 oz) creamy, soft goats' cheese

75 g (3 oz) Parmesan cheese, freshly grated

about 225 g (8 oz) smoked venison, Parma ham or smoked Black Forest ham

goats' cheese, to serve (optional)

1 Cook the spaghettini in boiling salted water for 10–12 minutes or until just tender.

2 Drain the spaghettini, toss in the tomatoes, oil and chives or onions, and return to the saucepan. Add the goats' cheese and fork through over a low heat. Add the Parmesan cheese. Taste and adjust the seasoning.

3 Put two or three slices of smoked meat on each plate. Add the hot spaghettini and serve immediately, accompanied by a little extra goats' cheese, if wished.

680 Calories per serving

NOT SUITABLE FOR FREEZING

Smoked Platter with Warm Pasta Salad (above)

FRESH RAVIOLI

SERVES 4

350 g (12 oz) fresh spinach, trimmed and washed
or 175 g (6 oz) frozen chopped spinach
175 g (6 oz) ricotta or curd cheese
125 g (4 oz) Parmesan cheese, freshly grated
1 egg, beaten
pinch of freshly grated nutmeg or ground allspice
salt and pepper
Home-made Pasta Dough made with 3 eggs and
300 g (11 oz) strong white flour (see page 8)
beaten egg or water for glazing
75 g (3 oz) butter
a few fresh sage leaves, chopped
fresh sage, to garnish

1 Place the spinach in a saucepan without any water, cover tightly and cook gently for 5–10 minutes, or until thawed if using frozen spinach. Drain very well and chop finely.

2 Mix together the spinach, ricotta or curd cheese, 65 g (2½ oz) of the Parmesan cheese, the egg, nutmeg or allspice and salt and pepper to taste.

3 Cut the dough in two. Wrap one half in cling film. Pat the other half out to a rectangle, then roll out firmly to an even sheet of almost paper-thin pasta. If it sticks, ease it carefully and dust with flour underneath. Make sure there are no holes or creases. Cover with a clean damp cloth and set aside while you roll out the other piece of dough in the same way.

4 Working quickly to prevent the pasta drying out, place teaspoonfuls of filling at 4 cm (1½ inch) intervals across and down the sheet of dough that has just been rolled out.

5 With a pastry brush or finger, glaze the spaces between the filling with beaten egg or water. This acts as a bond to seal the ravioli.

6 Uncover the other sheet of pasta, carefully lift this on the rolling pin and unroll it over the first sheet. Press down firmly around the pockets of filling and along the dampened lines to push out any trapped air and seal well.

7 With a ravioli cutter, serrated-edged wheel or a sharp knife, cut the ravioli into squares between the mounds of filling. Lift the ravioli one by one on to a well-floured baking sheet and leave to dry for about 1 hour before cooking. Alternatively, cover with cling film and refrigerate overnight.

8 Bring a large saucepan of lightly salted water to the boil. Add a few ravioli at a time and return to the boil. Cook for 3–5 minutes or until just tender.

9 Remove with a slotted spoon and place in a warmed buttered serving dish. Keep hot while cooking the remainder of the ravioli.

10 Melt the butter in a saucepan and stir in the rest of the grated Parmesan cheese with the chopped sage. Pour over the ravioli and toss to coat evenly. Serve immediately, garnished with fresh sage.

745 Calories per serving

SUITABLE FOR FREEZING

PASTA WITH COURGETTES AND BROAD BEANS

SERVES 2–3

175 g (6 oz) dried tagliatelle or spaghetti
salt and pepper
175 g (6 oz) courgettes, trimmed and thinly sliced
175 g (6 oz) frozen broad beans
150 g (5 oz) carton of full-fat soft cheese with
garlic and herbs
about 60 ml (4 tbsp) milk
or single cream
25 g (1 oz) pine kernels or walnut pieces, toasted

1 Cook the pasta in a large saucepan of boiling salted water for 3 minutes. Add the courgettes and

beans, and cook for a further 7 minutes or until the pasta is tender and the beans cooked. Drain well.

2 Return the pasta and vegetables to the pan and heat gently while stirring in the cheese and milk or cream. Add more milk if necessary. Season with salt and pepper.

3 Serve immediately, topped with the nuts.

810–540 Calories per serving

NOT SUITABLE FOR FREEZING

PARSLEYED LINGUINE WITH CLAMS AND SMOKED SALMON

SERVES 8

salt and pepper
15 ml (1 tbsp) vegetable oil
550 g (1¼ lb) fresh or 450 g (1 lb) dried linguine
75 g (3 oz) unsalted butter
1 garlic clove, skinned and crushed
45-60 ml (3–4 level tbsp) chopped fresh parsley or 30 ml (2 level tbsp) dried parsley
30 ml (2 tbsp) lemon juice
290 g (10 oz) can of baby clams in brine, drained and rinsed
225 g (8 oz) thinly sliced smoked salmon, cut in thin strips
15-30 ml (1–2 level tbsp) freshly grated Parmesan cheese

1 Bring a large saucepan of salted water to the boil. Add the oil and fresh or dried linguine. Return to the boil and cook until the pasta is just tender (3–4 minutes for fresh; 10–12 minutes for dried, or according to the packet instructions). Drain the pasta well.

2 Melt the butter in a large frying pan, add the garlic, parsley and pasta and toss together for 1 minute. Add the lemon juice and pepper (do not add any salt), then stir in the clams and smoked salmon and toss over a medium heat for 1–2 minutes or until heated through.

3 Sprinkle with Parmesan cheese and serve at once.

305 Calories per serving

NOT SUITABLE FOR FREEZING

PASTA SHELLS WITH CHEESE AND WALNUTS

SERVES 4

275 g (10 oz) dried pasta shells or other shapes
salt and pepper
25 g (1 oz) butter
250 g (9 oz) packet of mascarpone or other full-fat soft cheese
30 ml (2 level tbsp) freshly grated Parmesan cheese
75 g (3 oz) walnuts, roughly chopped

1 Cook the pasta shells in boiling salted water for 15–20 minutes or until just tender.

2 In another pan, melt the butter. Add the mascarpone cheese and stir for 2–3 minutes or until heated through. Do not boil.

3 Add the Parmesan cheese and walnuts and stir together. Drain the pasta well and add to the cheese mixture. Mix well until evenly coated with sauce. Season with salt and pepper, and serve immediately.

700 Calories per serving

NOT SUITABLE FOR FREEZING

*S*AUCES FOR PASTA

MEAT AND POULTRY

*C*LASSIC BOLOGNESE SAUCE

SERVES 4

50 g (2 oz) butter

125 g (4 oz) onion, skinned and finely chopped

50 g (2 oz) celery, trimmed and finely diced

50 g (2 oz) carrot, peeled and finely diced

350 g (12 oz) lean minced beef

50 g (2 oz) chorizo sausage or smoked streaky bacon, finely diced

100 ml (4 fl oz) milk

300 ml (10 fl oz) white wine

pinch of freshly grated nutmeg

1 bay leaf

30 ml (2 level tbsp) chopped fresh marjoram or thyme or 5 ml (1 level tsp) dried marjoram or thyme

400 g (14 oz) can of chopped tomatoes

25 g (1 oz) chopped sun-dried tomatoes

pinch of sugar

30 ml (2 level tbsp) tomato ketchup

salt and pepper

450 g (1 lb) fresh or dried pasta

1 Melt the butter in a heavy-based saucepan, add the onion and fry for about 5 minutes or until just translucent, stirring occasionally. Add the celery and carrot, and fry for a further 2 minutes.

2 Stir in the mince and sausage or bacon and continue cooking, stirring continuously, until the mince has changed colour and is free of lumps. Mix in the milk and cook for 4–5 minutes or until all the liquid has evaporated.

3 Add the wine, nutmeg, bay leaf, herbs, chopped tomatoes, sun-dried tomatoes, sugar and tomato ketchup. Add salt and pepper to taste. Return to the boil, then cover and cook over a low heat for about 1 hour or until well reduced and creamy, stirring occasionally.

4 About 15 minutes before the sauce is ready, cook the pasta in a large saucepan of boiling salted water for 2–4 minutes (for fresh pasta) or for 10–12 minutes (for dried pasta) or until just tender.

5 Add a little water to the sauce if very thick. Skim well. Taste and adjust the seasoning. Remove the bay leaf.

6 Drain the pasta, divide between warmed serving bowls and add the sauce. Serve immediately.

COOK'S TIPS

There are three essential points you must remember when making this Classic Bolognese Sauce.

1 The meat must be sautéed just long enough to lose its colour.

2 The meat is cooked in milk before the tomatoes or wine are added. You'll find that this keeps the meat creamier and sweeter tasting.

3 The sauce must cook at the lowest possible temperature for a long time. We've said an hour; the Bolognese would probably say at least three!

385 Calories per serving

SUITABLE FOR FREEZING AT THE END OF STEP 3

Classic Bolognese Sauce (above)

Simple Meat Sauce

Serves 12

45 ml (3 tbsp) vegetable oil
450 g (1 lb) onions, skinned and chopped
2 garlic cloves, skinned and crushed
1.4 kg (3 lb) lean minced beef
90 ml (6 tbsp) plain flour
three 400 g (14 oz) cans of chopped tomatoes
15 ml (1 level tbsp) tomato purée
about 600 ml (1 pint) beef stock
15 ml (1 level tbsp) dried mixed herbs
2 bay leaves
900 g (2 lb) fresh or dried pasta, to serve
salt and pepper

1 Heat the oil in a large saucepan or flameproof casserole, add the onions and garlic, and fry for about 5 minutes or until beginning to soften but not brown, stirring occasionally.
2 Add the minced beef and fry for 4–5 minutes, stirring occasionally to break up the minced beef.
3 Stir in the flour and cook, stirring, for 1–2 minutes. Add the remaining ingredients, except the pasta and seasoning.
4 Bring to the boil, then cover and simmer gently for about 1 hour, stirring occasionally. Top up with more stock if necessary.
5 About 15 minutes before the sauce is ready, cook the pasta in a large saucepan of boiling salted water for 2–4 minutes (for fresh pasta) or 10–12 minutes (for dried pasta) or until tender. Drain well.
6 Season the sauce with salt and pepper, remove the bay leaves and serve with the pasta.

565 Calories per serving

SUITABLE FOR FREEZING AT THE END OF STEP 4

Spaghetti with Lamb Ragu

Serves 4–6

45 ml (3 tbsp) olive oil
1 onion, skinned and finely chopped
2 garlic cloves, skinned and crushed
10 ml (2 level tsp) fennel seeds, lightly crushed
2 carrots, peeled and finely chopped
2 celery sticks, trimmed and finely chopped
350 g (12 oz) minced lamb
200 ml (7 fl oz) red wine
45 ml (3 level tbsp) chopped fresh oregano or
10 ml (2 level tsp) dried oregano
1 sprig of fresh rosemary
½ cinnamon stick
400 g (14 oz) can of chopped tomatoes
salt and pepper
400 g (14 oz) dried pasta, such as spaghetti or fettucine
75 ml (5 level tbsp) freshly grated Parmesan cheese, to serve

1 Heat the oil in a saucepan, add the onion and garlic, and cook over a medium heat for 5 minutes or until softened but not browned. Add the fennel seeds and cook for 1 minute, then add the carrots and celery and cook, stirring, for 2 minutes.
2 Add the lamb to the pan and cook for about 7 minutes or until browned. Increase the heat and stir in the wine. Cook for 4–5 minutes or until the liquid has reduced by about half.
3 Add the oregano, rosemary and cinnamon to the pan with the canned tomatoes. Bring to the boil and season with salt and pepper. Cook, uncovered, on a very low heat for 2½–3 hours or until the lamb is tender and the oil has separated from the sauce, stirring occasionally. Remove and discard the cinnamon stick and rosemary. Spoon off the oil, soaking up any excess with absorbent kitchen paper. Taste and adjust the seasoning.
4 Just before serving, cook the pasta in a large

saucepan of boiling salted water for 10–12 minutes or until just tender. Drain well.

5 To serve, toss the ragù with the pasta and about half of the grated Parmesan. Serve at once, sprinkled with the remaining Parmesan.

740–495 Calories per serving

SUITABLE FOR FREEZING AT THE END OF STEP 3

PASTA WITH SPICY SAUSAGE AND ROASTED TOMATO SAUCE

Serves 4

450 g (1 lb) tomatoes

30 ml (2 tbsp) vegetable oil

125 g (4 oz) onion, skinned and roughly chopped

10 ml (2 level tsp) dried oregano

1 garlic clove, skinned and crushed

450 g (1 lb) spicy pork sausages (see page 24), skinned (optional) and thickly sliced

15 ml (1 level tbsp) tomato purée

salt and pepper

Tabasco sauce, to taste

450 g (1 lb) dried orecchiette or cappalletti, to serve

1 Halve the tomatoes and scoop the seeds into a sieve over a small bowl. Press the seeds with a wooden spoon to extract all the juice. Discard the seeds and reserve the juice.

2 Place the tomatoes, skin side up, under a hot grill and cook until well browned and blistered. Leave until cool enough to handle, then rub to remove the skins. Roughly chop the flesh.

3 Heat the oil in a large saucepan and stir in the onion, oregano and garlic. Cook, stirring, for 2-3

minutes or until beginning to soften. Add the sliced sausages and continue to cook over a high heat until well browned.

4 Stir in the chopped tomatoes, reserved tomato juice and tomato purée. Season with salt and pepper, and add Tabasco sauce to taste. Bring to the boil, then reduce the heat, cover and simmer gently for 10–12 minutes. Taste and adjust the seasoning.

5 Meanwhile, cook the pasta in a large saucepan of boiling salted water for 10–12 minutes or until just tender. Drain well and divide between warmed serving bowls. Spoon over the sauce and serve at once.

930 Calories per serving

SUITABLE FOR FREEZING AT THE END OF STEP 4

VARIATION

For a quick alternative, use a 400 g (14 oz) can of chopped tomatoes instead of fresh tomatoes.

Sausage and Red Pesto Sauce

SERVES 4

450 g (1 lb) dried pasta
salt and pepper
30 ml (2 tbsp) olive oil
125 g (4 oz) onion, skinned and roughly chopped
1 garlic clove, skinned and crushed
1 red pepper, deseeded and sliced
400 g (14 oz) can of chopped tomatoes
30 ml (2 level tbsp) red pesto
5 ml (1 level tsp) sugar
350 g (12 oz) spicy Italian sausage
(see page 24), cooked and sliced
45 ml (3 level tbsp) freshly grated Parmesan
cheese
shavings of Parmesan cheese, to garnish

1 Cook the pasta in a large saucepan of boiling salted water for 10–12 minutes or until just tender. Drain well, and keep hot.
2 Meanwhile, heat the oil in a heavy-based frying pan, add the onion and garlic, and cook gently for 5-6 minutes or until soft and golden.
3 Add the sliced pepper, chopped tomatoes, pesto, sugar and sausage. Season with salt and pepper, mix well and bring to the boil. Reduce the heat and simmer gently for about 8 minutes.
4 Stir in the grated Parmesan cheese and serve immediately with hot cooked pasta. Garnish with Parmesan shavings.

COOK'S TIP

For a vegetarian dish, omit the spicy sausage and stir in cubes of feta cheese with the Parmesan.

680 Calories per serving

SAUCE SUITABLE FOR FREEZING AT THE END OF
STEP 3

Fusilli with Spicy Sausage

SERVES 6

45 ml (3 level tbsp) plain flour
salt and pepper
60 ml (4 tbsp) olive oil
275 g (10 oz) onion, skinned and finely chopped
1 large red chilli, finely chopped
2 garlic cloves, skinned and crushed
three 400 g (14 oz) cans of plum tomatoes
15 ml (1 level tbsp) sugar
500 g (1 lb 2 oz) spicy sausages (see page 24)
400 g (14 oz) dried fusilli

1 Season the flour with salt and pepper. Heat 30 ml (2 tbsp) oil in a frying pan, add the onion, chilli and garlic, and fry for 4–5 minutes or until soft and lightly coloured.
2 Drain the tomatoes, discarding the juice. Add the tomatoes and sugar to the onions and simmer slowly for 30 minutes or until the mixture is reduced by half.
3 Skin the sausages by running a knife down the length of each one and removing the meat. With wet hands, shape the sausage meat into walnut-sized balls and roll in the seasoned flour.
4 Heat the remaining oil in a frying pan and fry the meatballs in batches for 2–3 minutes or until golden brown. Do not worry if they break up a little. Drain on absorbent kitchen paper.
5 Add to the tomato sauce and simmer gently for another 15 minutes.
6 Meanwhile, cook the pasta in a large saucepan of boiling salted water for about 10 minutes or until just tender. Drain and return to the pan, add the meat and tomato sauce and stir thoroughly. Season to taste and serve.

710 Calories per serving

SUITABLE FOR FREEZING AT THE END OF STEP 5
WHEN COOL

*P*ASTA WITH PEPERAMI AND MUSHROOM

SERVES 3–4

175 g (6 oz) dried pasta shapes
salt and pepper
142 ml (5 fl oz) carton of soured cream
45 ml (3 tbsp) double cream
40 g (1½ oz) butter
175 g (6 oz) onions, skinned and thinly sliced
½ red pepper, deseeded and finely shredded
125 g (4 oz) button mushrooms, wiped
and quartered
two 25 g (1 oz) peperami sticks, thinly sliced
1 garlic clove, skinned and crushed
chopped fresh parsley, to garnish

1 Cook the pasta in a large saucepan of boiling salted water for 10–12 minutes or until just tender. Drain well.

2 Whisk together the soured cream, double cream and salt and pepper to taste.

3 Melt the butter in a large saucepan, add the onions and red pepper, cover and cook over a moderate heat until beginning to soften.

4 Increase the heat and stir in the mushrooms, peperami, pasta and garlic. Stir over a high heat until all the ingredients are piping hot.

5 Remove from the heat and immediately stir in the cream mixture. There should be sufficient heat to warm the cream mixture. If not, stir over a gentle heat for a further few seconds to warm through.

6 Garnish with the chopped parsley and serve immediately.

585–440 Calories per serving

NOT SUITABLE FOR FREEZING

*S*PAGHETTI MILANESE

SERVES 4

25 g (1 oz) butter or margarine
1 medium onion, skinned and chopped
50 g (2 oz) mushrooms, wiped and chopped
450 g (1 lb) tomatoes, skinned and chopped, or
400 g (14 oz) can of chopped tomatoes
1 bay leaf
pinch of dried thyme
pinch of freshly grated nutmeg
5 ml (1 level tsp) sugar
salt and pepper
50 g (2 oz) ham, chopped
50 g (2 oz) tongue, chopped
450-700 g (1–1½ lb) dried spaghetti
freshly grated Parmesan cheese, to serve

1 Melt the butter or margarine in a large saucepan, add the onion and mushrooms, and fry for 3–5 minutes or until soft.

2 Stir in the tomatoes, herbs, nutmeg and sugar. Season with salt and pepper, cover and simmer gently for about 20 minutes or until the sauce has thickened.

3 Add the ham and tongue and simmer, uncovered, for a further 5–10 minutes. Remove the bay leaf.

4 Cook the spaghetti in a large saucepan of boiling salted water for 10–12 minutes or until just tender. Drain well, return to the pan and mix with the sauce.

5 Pour into a warmed serving dish. Serve the cheese in a separate dish.

715 Calories per serving

NOT SUITABLE FOR FREEZING

23

Pasta with Mushroom and Leek Sauce

Serves 4

450 g (1 lb) dried pasta, such as
pappardelle or linguine
salt and pepper
25 g (1 oz) butter or margarine
225 g (8 oz) mushrooms, wiped and thinly sliced
125 g (4 oz) leeks, trimmed, thinly sliced and
washed
125 g (4 oz) pancetta or unsmoked streaky
bacon, derinded and roughly chopped
1 garlic clove, skinned and crushed
125 g (4 oz) full-fat soft cheese with garlic and
herbs
30 ml (2 tbsp) milk or single cream

1 Cook the pasta in a large saucepan of boiling salted water for 10–12 minutes or until just tender.

2 Meanwhile, melt the butter or margarine in a saucepan and stir in the mushrooms, leeks, pancetta or bacon and garlic. Fry for 3–4 minutes or until the leeks are tender but still retain some bite, stirring continuously.

3 Lower the heat and stir in the soft cheese and milk or cream until thoroughly mixed. Season with salt and pepper. Drain the pasta thoroughly and toss with the mushroom and leek sauce. Serve immediately.

650 Calories per serving

NOT SUITABLE FOR FREEZING

Spicy Sausage and Chicken Liver Pasta Sauce

Serves 4

225 g (8 oz) coarse spicy pork sausages
(see Cook's tip)
350 g (12 oz) chicken livers, thawed if frozen
45 ml (3 tbsp) olive oil
25 g (1 oz) butter
125 g (4 oz) onion, skinned and chopped
300 ml (½ pint) passata
150 ml (5 fl oz) dry white wine
salt and pepper
45 ml (3 level tbsp) chopped fresh parsley
350 g (12 oz) dried pasta
freshly grated Parmesan cheese, to serve

1 Skin the sausages and roughly crumble the meat. Trim and halve the chicken livers.

2 Heat the oil and butter in a frying pan, add the chicken livers and fry until brown. Remove the livers with a slotted spoon. Stir in the onion and cook for about 5 minutes or until softened.

3 Add the sausage meat and cook over a high heat until well browned, stirring well.

4 Stir in the passata and wine, and bring to the boil, then reduce the heat, cover and simmer for 10–15 minutes. Add the chicken livers, cover and cook for 10 minutes.

5 Cook the pasta in boiling salted water for 10–12 minutes or until just tender. Drain well.

6 Season the sauce with salt and pepper, and stir in the chopped fresh parsley. Toss the hot cooked pasta with Parmesan cheese and spoon the sauce on top. Serve at once.

COOK'S TIP

These coarse, spicy sausages are found in good delicatessens and have a firmer texture than traditional pork sausages. Or you could replace them with 75 g (3 oz) chopped coarse salami, stirring this in just before serving.

800 Calories per serving

SUITABLE FOR FREEZING AT THE END OF STEP 4

———————— ❧ ————————

CHICKEN LIVER BOLOGNESE

SERVES 4

225 g (8 oz) chicken livers, thawed if frozen
30 ml (2 tbsp) olive oil
125 g (4 oz) onion, skinned and chopped
125 g (4 oz) smoked streaky bacon, derinded and chopped
450 g (1 lb) lean minced beef
400 g (14 oz) can of chopped tomatoes
150 ml (5 fl oz) dry red wine
10 ml (2 level tsp) dried oregano or dried mixed herbs
30 ml (2 level tbsp) tomato purée
salt and pepper
450 g (1 lb) dried spaghetti or tagliatelle or other noodles

1 Trim and roughly chop the chicken livers.
2 Heat the oil in a medium saucepan, add the onion, bacon, chicken livers and beef, and fry for 4–5 minutes or until the meat breaks up, stirring all the time.
3 Add the remaining ingredients, except the pasta, cover and simmer for 25–30 minutes.
4 Cook the pasta in a large saucepan of boiling salted water for 10–12 minutes or until just tender. Drain well.
5 Divide the pasta between four heated serving plates and spoon the chicken liver mixture on top.

580 Calories per serving

NOT SUITABLE FOR FREEZING

PASTA WITH PEPPERED BEEF

SERVES 2–3

350 g (12 oz) sirloin steaks
10 ml (2 tsp) green peppercorns in brine, drained
225 g (8 oz) dried pasta shapes
salt
30 ml (2 tbsp) olive oil
175 g (6 oz) red onion, skinned and thinly sliced
90 ml (6 tbsp) smetana or natural low-fat yogurt
15 ml (1 tbsp) lemon juice
lemon slices, to garnish

1 Cut the steaks into fine, thin strips. Finely chop the peppercorns.
2 Cook the pasta in a large saucepan of boiling salted water for 10–12 minutes or until just tender.
3 Meanwhile, heat the oil in a frying pan, add the onion and fry until just beginning to soften.
4 Stir in the beef and peppercorns and cook over a high heat for 2–3 minutes or until the meat is tender, stirring frequently.
5 Lower the heat and stir in the smetana or yogurt and lemon juice with salt to taste. To serve, drain the pasta, divide it between warmed serving bowls and spoon over the sauce. Garnish with lemon slices.

915–610 Calories per serving

NOT SUITABLE FOR FREEZING

———————— ❧ ————————

*P*APPARDELLE WITH FRAZZLED PROSCIUTTO AND ASPARAGUS SAUCE

SERVES 4–6

350 g (12 oz) frozen broad beans, thawed
350 g (12 oz) asparagus
90 ml (6 tbsp) olive oil
175 g (6 oz) prosciutto (Parma ham), in thin slices
3 shallots, skinned and finely chopped
2 garlic cloves, skinned and crushed
400 g (14 oz) dried pappardelle noodles
salt and pepper
45 ml (3 level tbsp) chopped fresh parsley
300 g (11 oz) goats' cheese 'log' (with rind), sliced

1 Skin the broad beans, if wished, and set aside.
2 Trim the asparagus and cut into 5 cm (2 inch) lengths. Cook in shallow, boiling water for 2–3 minutes or until almost tender. Drain and refresh.
3 Heat the oil in a frying pan. Add the prosciutto in batches and fry over a high heat for a few seconds. Lift out on to a plate and set aside.
4 Add the shallots and garlic to the pan and cook for 5 minutes to soften, but without browning. Increase the heat and add the beans. Cook, stirring, for 2 minutes.
5 Cook the pasta in a large saucepan of boiling salted water for 10–12 minutes or until just tender.
6 Meanwhile, preheat the grill. Add the asparagus to the shallot mixture with the parsley. Cook, stirring, for 2 minutes, then return the prosciutto to the pan. Season with salt and pepper.
7 Drain the pasta and toss it with the prosciutto mixture in a heatproof bowl. Top with sliced goats' cheese and grill for 2–3 minutes or until lightly browned. Serve at once.

850–565 Calories per serving

NOT SUITABLE FOR FREEZING

*T*AGLIATELLE WITH PROSCIUTTO, PEAS AND CREAM SAUCE

SERVES 4

225–350 g (8–12 oz) dried tagliatelle
salt and pepper
50 g (2 oz) butter or margarine
1 large onion, skinned and finely sliced
125 g (4 oz) prosciutto (Parma ham), in thin slices
125 g (4 oz) peas, cooked
60 ml (4 tbsp) single cream
50 g (2 oz) Parmesan cheese, freshly grated

1 Cook the pasta in a large saucepan of boiling salted water for 10–12 minutes or until just tender.
2 Melt the butter or margarine in a saucepan, add the onion and cook for about 3 minutes or until the onion is soft. Add the prosciutto and peas, and cook for a further 5 minutes.
3 Drain the pasta and add it to the prosciutto mixture. Stir well, then add the cream and half the cheese. Toss gently, add salt and pepper to taste, and serve at once in a warmed serving dish with the remaining cheese in a separate bowl.

545 Calories per serving

NOT SUITABLE FOR FREEZING

Pappardelle with Frazzled Prosciutto and Asparagus Sauce (above)

*I*TALIAN-STYLE MEATBALLS

SERVES 4

30 ml (2 tbsp) olive oil

1 large onion, skinned and finely chopped

2 garlic cloves, skinned and crushed

400 g (14 oz) can of chopped tomatoes

10 ml (2 level tsp) dried mixed herbs

10 ml (2 level tsp) dried oregano

salt and pepper

450 g (1 lb) lean minced beef

50 g (2 oz) fresh white breadcrumbs

50 g (2 oz) Parmesan cheese, freshly grated

1 egg, beaten

20 small stoned black olives

vegetable oil for deep-frying

100 ml (4 fl oz) red or white dry Italian wine

about 300 ml (½ pint) water

225 g (8 oz) dried tagliatelle or spaghetti

1 Heat the oil in a heavy-based saucepan and add the onion and half the garlic. Fry gently for 5 minutes or until lightly coloured.

2 Add the tomatoes, half the herbs and salt and pepper to taste. Bring to the boil, stirring, then lower the heat, cover and simmer for about 20 minutes.

3 Meanwhile, make the meatballs. Put the minced beef in a bowl with the breadcrumbs, Parmesan cheese, remaining garlic and remaining herbs. Mix well with your hands, then add salt and pepper to taste and bind with the beaten egg.

4 Pick up a small amount of the mixture, about the size of a walnut. Press one olive in the centre, then shape the mixture around it. Repeat with the remaining olives and meat to make 20 meatballs.

5 Heat the vegetable oil in a deep-fat fryer to 190°C (375°F). Deep-fry the meatballs in batches for 2–3 minutes or until lightly browned, then drain thoroughly on absorbent kitchen paper.

6 Stir the wine into the tomato sauce, then add the water and meatballs. Shake the pan to coat the balls in the sauce, adding more water if necessary. Cover and simmer for 15 minutes.

7 Meanwhile, cook the pasta in a large saucepan of boiling salted water for 10–12 minutes or until just tender. Drain, place in a large, warmed serving bowl, and spoon the meatballs and sauce over the top. Serve at once.

715 Calories per serving

SAUCE SUITABLE FOR FREEZING

*M*EATBALL AND MUSHROOM SAUCE

SERVES 4

450 g (1 lb) lean minced beef

50 g (2 oz) fresh white or wholemeal breadcrumbs

50 g (2 oz) onion, skinned and finely chopped

50 g (2 oz) mature Cheddar cheese, grated

2.5 ml (½ level tsp) ready-made mild mustard

salt and pepper

1 egg, beaten

30 ml (2 tbsp) vegetable oil

400 g (14 oz) can of cream of mushroom soup

225 g (8 oz) wholewheat spaghetti

1 Mix together the minced beef, breadcrumbs, onion, cheese and mustard. Season well with salt and pepper, and bind with the beaten egg. (You can do this in a food processor but be careful not to overblend.)

2 Turn the meat mixture out on to a lightly floured board. Using floured hands, divide the mixture into 16 and roll each piece into a ball.

3 Heat the oil in a frying pan, add half the meatballs and fry until browned, turning frequently.

Remove from the pan and drain on absorbent kitchen paper. Repeat with the remaining meat-balls.

4 Pour the excess fat out of the frying pan and wipe out with kitchen paper. Replace the meat-balls, pour the soup over and season with pepper. Cover and simmer gently for 20–30 minutes or until tender.

5 Cook the spaghetti in a large saucepan of boil-ing salted water for 10–12 minutes or until just tender. Drain well and divide between warmed serving bowls. Spoon over the meatball sauce and serve at once.

670 Calories per serving

SAUCE SUITABLE FOR FREEZING

---

*P*ORK AND PASTA STIR-FRY

SERVES 4

450 g (1 lb) pork tenderloin (fillet)

75 g (3 oz) streaky bacon, derinded and chopped

225 g (8 oz) onions (preferably red), skinned and finely sliced

15 ml (1 level tbsp) wholegrain mustard

100 ml (4 fl oz) dry cider

1 garlic clove, skinned and crushed

45 ml (3 tbsp) vegetable oil

salt and pepper

175 g (6 oz) green beans, topped, tailed and halved

1 green pepper, deseeded and cut into strips

75 g (3 oz) dried pasta shells or bows

15 ml (1 tbsp) soy sauce

60 ml (4 tbsp) stock

1 Cut the pork into strips, about 5 cm x 5 mm (2 x ¼ inch), discarding skin and excess fat. Place in a bowl with the bacon and onions. Add the mus-tard, cider, garlic, 15 ml (1 tbsp) oil, and salt and pepper to taste. Stir well, cover and leave to mari-nate in the refrigerator for at least 1 hour, prefer-ably overnight.

2 Blanch the green beans and pepper together in boiling salted water for 2 minutes. Drain, refresh under cold running water, and leave until cool.

3 Cook the pasta in a large saucepan of boiling salted water for 10–12 minutes or until just ten-der. Drain well.

4 Drain the meat and the onions from the mari-nade, reserving the juices. Heat the remaining oil in a large frying pan, add the meat and onions and stir-fry over a high heat for 3–4 minutes or until the meat is lightly browned and the onions are beginning to soften.

5 Put the beans, pepper and pasta into the pan with the reserved marinade, the soy sauce and stock. Season with salt and pepper. Bring to the boil, stirring, then reduce the heat and simmer for about 5 minutes or until piping hot.

545 Calories per serving

NOT SUITABLE FOR FREEZING

Pasta with Pork, Sage and Feta Cheese

SERVES 4

450 g (1 lb) pork fillet
125 g (4 oz) feta cheese
30 ml (2 level tbsp) chopped fresh sage or
2.5 ml (½ level tsp) dried sage
60 ml (4 level tbsp) chopped fresh parsley
salt and pepper
50 g (2 oz) butter
125 g (4 oz) onion, skinned and chopped
150 ml (5 fl oz) white wine
150 ml (5 fl oz) chicken stock
150 ml (5 fl oz) crème fraîche
350 g (12 oz) dried pasta ribbons, such as
pappardelle or tagliatelle
butter, to serve

1 Cut the pork into four pieces. Place between sheets of greaseproof paper and bat out with a mallet or rolling pin until 3 mm (⅛ inch) thick.
2 Blend the feta with 15 ml (1 level tbsp) sage and 30 ml (2 level tbsp) parsley. Season.
3 Spread the pork with the cheese mixture. Roll up each piece and skewer with a cocktail stick.
4 Melt the butter in a frying pan, add the onion, and fry for 4–5 minutes or until softened. Add the pork and fry for 2–3 minutes or until browned.
5 Pour in the wine and stock, and bring to the boil. Add the remaining herbs and the crème fraîche, cover and simmer for 10–15 minutes or until the pork is tender.
6 Meanwhile, cook the pasta in boiling salted water for 10–12 minutes. Drain, toss in butter, season and arrange on a serving dish.
7 Remove the pork from the sauce and slice. Arrange the slices on top of the pasta and pour over the sauce. Serve at once.

515 Calories per serving

NOT SUITABLE FOR FREEZING

Spaghetti with Bacon Ragu

SERVES 6

45 ml (3 tbsp) olive oil
225 g (8 oz) onions, skinned and sliced
1 garlic clove, skinned and crushed
750 g (1½ lb) lean collar bacon, very finely
chopped
30 ml (2 level tbsp) plain flour
75 ml (5 level tbsp) tomato purée
10 ml (2 level tsp) dried sage
450 g (1 lb) tomatoes, peeled, deseeded and
quartered
50 ml (2 fl oz) dry white wine
450 ml (¾ pint) unseasoned stock
salt and pepper
350 g (12 oz) dried spaghetti
25 g (1 oz) butter

1 Heat the oil in a large, heavy-based saucepan, add the onions and fry for 5–10 minutes. Add the garlic and fry for a further 1 minute, then stir in the bacon and fry, stirring, for 5 minutes.
2 Sprinkle over the flour and cook, stirring, for 1 minute. Add the tomato purée, sage and tomatoes and mix well, then stir in the wine and stock. Season well with salt and pepper, then bring to the boil, stirring. Reduce the heat and simmer, uncovered, for about 1¼ hours or until the mixture is reduced by half and the meat is tender.
3 About 15 minutes before the ragu is ready, cook the spaghetti in a large saucepan of boiling salted water for 10–12 minutes or until tender. Drain well and return to the saucepan with the butter. Toss until the butter has melted and all the spaghetti strands are coated.
4 Pile the spaghetti in a warmed serving dish and pour over the bacon ragu. Serve immediately.

595 Calories per serving

RAGU SUITABLE FOR FREEZING

*B*RANDIED CHICKEN

SERVES 4

25 g (1 oz) butter

4 chicken breast fillets, about 125 g
(4 oz) each, skinned

75 g (3 oz) shallots or onions, skinned and
finely chopped

200 ml (7 fl oz) lager

25 ml (1 fl oz) brandy

175 g (6 oz) button mushrooms, wiped

50 ml (2 fl oz) double cream

salt and pepper

350 g (12 oz) dried pasta noodles, such as
fettucine or tagliatelle

flat-leafed parsley, to garnish

1 Melt the butter in a flameproof casserole, add two of the chicken breasts and fry until browned. Remove with a slotted spoon and brown the remaining two chicken breasts.

2 Stir the shallots or onions into the pan and fry for 1–2 minutes, stirring. Return all the chicken to the pan and add the lager, brandy and mushrooms. Bring to the boil, then reduce the heat, cover and simmer for about 20 minutes or until the chicken is very tender.

3 Remove the chicken from the pan, cover with foil and keep warm. Boil the cooking liquor until reduced by half, then stir in the cream and season with salt and pepper.

4 Cook the pasta in a large saucepan of boiling salted water for 10–12 minutes or until just tender. Drain well.

5 Arrange the pasta in a warmed serving dish, place the chicken breasts on top and pour over the sauce. Garnish with parsley and serve at once.

620 Calories per serving

NOT SUITABLE FOR FREEZING

*T*URKEY PAPRIKA WITH PASTA

SERVES 4

15 ml (1 tbsp) olive oil

1 small onion, skinned and sliced

450 g (1 lb) boneless turkey breast,
skinned and cut into strips

15 ml (1 level tbsp) paprika

450 ml (¾ pint) chicken stock

salt and pepper

1 green pepper, deseeded and sliced

125 g (4 oz) small wholemeal pasta shapes,
such as spirals

30 ml (2 tbsp) soured cream

fresh parsley and paprika, to garnish

1 Heat the oil in a large frying pan, add the onion and fry for 5 minutes or until golden.

2 Add the turkey and paprika to the pan and stir over a moderate heat for 2 minutes.

3 Stir in the stock, season with salt and pepper and bring to the boil. Add the green pepper and pasta, cover and simmer gently for 15–20 minutes or until the turkey and pasta are tender.

4 Stir in the soured cream and adjust the seasoning. Garnish with parsley and a little paprika, then serve immediately.

COOK'S TIP

Paprika is a red powder prepared from dried sweet peppers from Spain and Hungary. The flavour can vary from mild to hot. The best quality paprika is mild, sweet and bright red.

310 Calories per serving

NOT SUITABLE FOR FREEZING

Liver goujons with orange sauce

Serves 4

350 g (12 oz) lamb's liver, sliced
75 ml (5 level tbsp) plain flour
salt and pepper
1 egg, beaten
125 g (4 oz) medium oatmeal
50 g (2 oz) butter or margarine
1 medium onion, skinned and sliced
300 ml (½ pint) lamb or beef stock
juice and finely grated rind of 1 medium orange
5 ml (1 level tsp) dried sage
a few drops of gravy browning
350 g (12 oz) dried pasta shapes
60 ml (4 tbsp) vegetable oil

1 Cut the liver into 5 cm (2 inch) strips. Season 45 ml (3 tbsp) flour and toss with the liver until coated. Dip the liver in beaten egg and coat with oatmeal. Chill in the refrigerator.
2 Fry the onion in 25 g (1 oz) butter until golden brown. Add the remaining flour and cook, stirring, for 1–2 minutes. Gradually blend in the stock, orange rind and juice and sage. Season, bring to the boil and simmer for 10–15 minutes, stirring constantly. Add the gravy browning and taste and adjust the seasoning.
3 Cook the pasta in boiling salted water for 10–12 minutes or until just tender.
4 Meanwhile, heat the remaining butter and the oil in a frying pan and fry the liver gently for 1–2 minutes or until tender.
5 Drain the pasta and tip into a warmed serving dish. Arrange the liver on top. Pour a little of the sauce over the liver and pasta; serve the remainder separately.

610 Calories per serving

NOT SUITABLE FOR FREEZING

Lamb's liver and mushrooms

Serves 3

350 g (12 oz) dried pasta shapes
15 g (½ oz) butter or margarine
1 medium onion, skinned and sliced
450 g (1 lb) lamb's liver, sliced
15 ml (1 level tbsp) plain flour
125 g (4 oz) button mushrooms, wiped
150 ml (5 fl oz) beef stock
4 tomatoes, skinned and roughly chopped
30 ml (2 tbsp) Worcestershire sauce
salt and pepper
150 ml (5 fl oz) soured cream

1 Cook the pasta in a large saucepan of boiling salted water for 10–12 minutes or until just tender.
2 Meanwhile, melt the butter or margarine in a large frying pan, add the onion, and fry gently for 5 minutes or until soft.
3 Cut the liver into thin strips, sprinkle with the flour and toss until coated. Add to the pan with the mushrooms. Fry for 5 minutes, stirring well, then add the stock and bring to the boil.
4 Stir in the tomatoes and Worcestershire sauce. Season with salt and pepper, then simmer for 3–4 minutes. Stir in the soured cream and reheat without boiling.
5 Drain the pasta and tip into a warmed serving dish. Pour over the liver and mushrooms, and serve at once.

465 Calories per serving

NOT SUITABLE FOR FREEZING

SPICED LIVER SAUTE

SERVES 4

30 ml (2 tbsp) olive oil
450 g (1 lb) lamb's liver, cut into thin strips
125 g (4 oz) onion, skinned and sliced
125 g (4 oz) button mushrooms, wiped and sliced
125 g (4 oz) fine green beans, topped and tailed
15 ml (1 level tbsp) plain flour
5–10 ml (1–2 level tsp) paprika
salt and pepper
450 g (1 lb) dried pasta noodles, such as tagliatelle
150 ml (5 fl oz) vegetable stock
Tabasco sauce, to taste
150 ml (5 fl oz) single cream

1 Heat the oil in a large frying pan and fry the liver, stirring, until browned. Lift out with a slotted spoon, set aside and keep warm.

2 Add the onion, mushrooms and beans to the pan with a little more oil if necessary, and cook, stirring, for about 5 minutes or until beginning to soften. Mix in the flour and paprika and cook for a further 1 minute.

3 Cook the pasta in a large saucepan of boiling salted water for 10–12 minutes or until just tender.

4 Add the stock, liver and Tabasco to taste to the vegetables. Season with salt and pepper, cover and simmer for 5–10 minutes or until the liver is cooked and the vegetables are just tender.

5 Stir in the cream, taste and adjust the seasoning and bubble up quickly.

6 Drain the pasta well and divide between four heated serving plates. Serve the spicy liver mixture with the pasta.

765 Calories per serving

NOT SUITABLE FOR FREEZING

CALF'S LIVER AND CREAM SAUCE

SERVES 2

175–225 g (6–8 oz) dried pasta
salt and pepper
15 ml (1 level tbsp) plain flour
2.5 ml (½ level tsp) paprika
4 slices of calf's liver, about 225 g (8 oz)
knob of butter
30 ml (2 tbsp) dry white wine
60 ml (4 tbsp) single cream
15 ml (1 level tbsp) chopped fresh parsley

1 Cook the pasta in a large saucepan of boiling salted water for 10–12 minutes or until just tender.

2 Meanwhile, put the flour in a polythene bag and add the paprika. (Do not add salt as this will toughen the liver.) Add the liver and shake well to coat each piece.

3 Heat the butter in a frying pan. Add the liver and fry over medium heat for 2–3 minutes on each side. Remove from the pan and keep warm.

4 Add the wine to the pan and boil briskly for 1 minute, stirring in any sediment from the bottom of the pan. Lower the heat, stir in the cream and parsley, and season with salt and pepper. Heat gently without boiling.

5 Drain the pasta and put in a warmed serving dish, arrange the liver pieces on top and pour over the sauce. Serve at once.

VARIATION

Substitute lamb's liver for calf's liver if you prefer it, or cannot buy calf's liver.

690 Calories per serving

NOT SUITABLE FOR FREEZING

Sauces for Pasta

Fish and Shellfish

Seafood Spaghetti

SERVES 4–6

900 g (2 lb) fresh mussels
30 ml (2 tbsp) olive oil
2 leeks, trimmed, thinly sliced and washed
1 onion, skinned and finely chopped
1 garlic clove, skinned and crushed
large pinch of saffron strands
350 g (12 oz) dried spaghetti
salt and pepper
200 ml (7 fl oz) dry white wine
150 ml (5 fl oz) double cream
45 ml (3 level tbsp) chopped fresh parsley
225 g (8 oz) large cooked peeled prawns
175 g (6 oz) scallops, cleaned (optional)
chopped fresh parsley, to garnish

1 Discard any cracked mussels and any that remain open when tapped smartly on the shell. Scrub the mussels, pull off the coarse threads (beards) from the sides of the shells, and soak in cold water with a little salt and oatmeal for at least 30 minutes and up to 2 hours.

2 Heat the oil in a large saucepan, add the leeks, onion, garlic and saffron, and fry for 3–4 minutes,

stirring all the time. Cover the pan, lower the heat and cook for about 10 minutes or until the vegetables are very soft.

3 Cook the spaghetti in a large saucepan of boiling salted water for 8–10 minutes or until just tender.

4 Meanwhile, add the wine, cream and parsley to the leek mixture. Bring to the boil and boil for a few minutes to reduce slightly.

5 Drain the mussels and add them to the leek mixture with the prawns and scallops, if using. Re-cover and cook for 2–3 minutes, shaking the pan frequently, until the mussels have opened. Discard any mussels that stay closed.

6 Drain the spaghetti, toss with the seafood sauce and season with salt and pepper. Serve immediately, garnished with plenty of chopped parsley.

745–495 Calories per serving

NOT SUITABLE FOR FREEZING

Seafood Spaghetti

SHELLFISH PASTA WITH ROAST CHERRY TOMATOES

SERVES 6

6 medium onions, skinned
450 g (1 lb) cherry tomatoes
75 ml (5 tbsp) olive oil
15 ml (1 level tbsp) chopped fresh thyme
salt and pepper
3-4 garlic cloves, skinned and crushed
175 ml (6 fl oz) dry white wine
parsley stalks
900 g (2 lb) mixed prepared and cooked seafood,
such as prawns, mussels and squid
400 g (14 oz) dried spaghetti
chopped fresh parsley, to garnish

1 Preheat the oven to 200°C (400°F) mark 6. Cut each onion into six wedges, leaving the root end intact. Arrange in one layer in a roasting tin. Halve the cherry tomatoes and arrange, cut-side up, in the tin. Drizzle 45 ml (3 tbsp) of the olive oil over and sprinkle with thyme, salt and pepper. Roast in the oven for 45 minutes or until the onions are tender and the tomatoes soft.

2 Meanwhile, heat the remaining oil in a large saucepan. Add the garlic and cook over a medium heat for 1 minute. Add the wine and parsley stalks, bring to the boil and cook for 2 minutes. Add the seafood and simmer for 3–4 minutes or until heated through.

3 About 10–15 minutes before serving, cook the pasta in boiling salted water until almost tender. Drain the pasta thoroughly, then return it to the pan. Add the shellfish and the roasted onion and tomato mixture and toss lightly. Taste and adjust the seasoning and serve at once, garnished with chopped parsley.

760 Calories per serving

NOT SUITABLE FOR FREEZING

VARIATION

This recipe is also delicious made with fish. Use 450 g (1 lb) skinless salmon fillet and 450 g (1 lb) skinless cod fillets instead of the mixed seafood. Dice the fish into bite-sized pieces. Follow the instructions as for seafood in step 2 but cook for 5–7 minutes. Use 15 ml (1 level tbsp) chopped fresh dill instead of thyme.

TAGLIATELLE WITH SEAFOOD AND CHAMPAGNE SAUCE

SERVES 4

16 fresh mussels
175 g (6 oz) fresh clams
150 ml (5 fl oz) fish stock
one 300 g (11 oz) red mullet, filleted
175 g (6 oz) salmon fillets, skinned
4 large uncooked Pacific prawns, peeled and deveined
4 fresh scallops, shelled
225 g (8 oz) fresh tagliatelle
salt and pepper
75 g (3 oz) butter
50 g (2 oz) leek, trimmed, cut into fine julienne strips and washed
150 ml (5 fl oz) champagne or sparkling dry white wine
300 ml (10 fl oz) double cream
pinch of cayenne
12 fresh basil leaves

1 Prepare the mussels and clams as described on page 34, discarding any which do not close when tapped. Place in a pan with the stock, cover and cook for 2–3 minutes or until the shells open. Discard any closed shells. Leave to cool, then remove the mussels and clams from their shells. Strain the stock and reserve.

2 Cut the fish into 1 cm (½ inch) strips. Cut each prawn in half. Separate the coral from each scallop and cut the scallops in half crossways.

3 Cook the tagliatelle in boiling salted water for 2–3 minutes. Drain and toss in half the butter. Season with salt and pepper.

4 Melt the remaining butter in a saucepan, add the leek, prawns, scallop and scallop coral, and fry for 30 seconds. Add the fish fillets, champagne and reserved stock, and simmer for 1 minute. Remove the fish from the pan and keep warm.

5 Boil the cooking liquid rapidly until reduced by half. Add the cream and boil until thick. Season with salt and pepper, and add the cayenne. Return the fish to the sauce with the seafood and basil. Warm through, then serve with the tagliatelle.

1000 Calories per serving

NOT SUITABLE FOR FREEZING

*F*ETTUCCINE WITH CLAM SAUCE

SERVES 4

15 ml (1 tbsp) olive oil

1 medium onion, skinned and finely chopped

2–3 garlic cloves, skinned and crushed

700 g (1½ lb) tomatoes, skinned and roughly chopped, or one 400 g (14 oz) and one 225 g (8 oz) can of tomatoes

two 200 g (7 oz) cans or jars of baby clams in brine, drained

30 ml (2 level tbsp) chopped fresh parsley

salt and pepper

400 g (14 oz) fettuccine or other long thin pasta, preferably wholewheat

1 To make the sauce, heat the oil in a saucepan, add the onion and garlic and fry gently for 5 minutes or until soft but not coloured.

2 Stir in the tomatoes and their juice, bring to the boil and cook for 15–20 minutes or until slightly reduced.

3 Stir the drained clams into the sauce with half of the parsley and salt and pepper to taste. Remove from the heat.

4 Cook the fettuccine in a large saucepan of boiling salted water for 8–10 minutes or until just tender.

5 Reheat the sauce just before the pasta is cooked. Drain the fettuccine well, tip it into a warmed serving dish and pour over the clam sauce. Sprinkle with the remaining chopped parsley to garnish.

510 Calories per serving

NOT SUITABLE FOR FREEZING

VARIATION

Replace the clams with canned mussels, or mussels in jars.

PASTA WITH PRAWNS, MUSHROOMS AND WINE

SERVES 4–6

15 g (½ oz) dried porcini mushrooms
25 g (1 oz) butter
60 ml (4 tbsp) olive oil
1 onion, skinned and finely chopped
2 garlic cloves, skinned and crushed
150 ml (5 fl oz) dry white wine
400 g (14 oz) dried pasta shapes
salt and pepper
4 tomatoes, skinned, deseeded and diced
16 cooked peeled tiger prawns
30 ml (2 level tbsp) chopped fresh parsley
tarragon leaves, to garnish (optional)

1 Soak the mushrooms in 150 ml (5 fl oz) boiling water for 2 minutes. Drain, reserving the liquor. Rinse the mushrooms and chop finely.
2 Heat the butter and oil in a frying pan, add the onion and cook for 5 minutes or until soft but not browned. Stir in the garlic and cook for 1 minute, then add the mushrooms. Cook for a few seconds, then add the wine and the reserved mushroom liquor.
3 Cook the pasta in boiling salted water for 10–12 minutes or until just tender. Drain well.
4 Return the mushroom mixture to the boil and bubble until the liquid is reduced by half, then add the tomatoes and prawns, and season with salt and pepper.
5 Mix the sauce and parsley in with the pasta. Serve sprinkled with tarragon leaves, if wished.

675–450 Calories per serving

NOT SUITABLE FOR FREEZING

CREAMY PASTA WITH PRAWNS

SERVES 4

225 g (8 oz) dried pasta shells or spirals
salt and pepper
15 ml (1 tbsp) vegetable oil
75 g (3 oz) spring onions, trimmed and sliced
1 garlic clove, skinned and crushed
5 ml (1 level tsp) tomato purée
90 ml (6 tbsp) fromage frais or single cream
125 g (4 oz) cooked peeled prawns
200 g (7 oz) can of tuna steaks in brine, drained and flaked
small bunch of fresh basil, chopped
60 ml (4 tbsp) water
spring onion shreds and basil, to garnish (optional)

1 Cook the pasta in a large saucepan of boiling salted water for 10–12 minutes or until just tender.
2 Meanwhile, heat the oil in a medium saucepan, add the onions and garlic, and fry for 1 minute, stirring. Stir in the tomato purée, fromage frais or single cream, prawns and tuna with a little chopped fresh basil and the water, and simmer for 2–3 minutes to heat through.
3 Drain the pasta thoroughly, then return it to the pan. Pour over the sauce, stirring to mix. Warm gently to heat through, then taste and adjust the seasoning. Garnish with spring onion shreds and basil, if wished.

385 Calories per serving

NOT SUITABLE FOR FREEZING

Pasta with Prawns, Mushrooms and Wine

Mussel and Tomato Sauce with Pasta

Serves 4

225 g (8 oz) fine tagliatelle (tagliolini)
salt and pepper
2 bunches of spring onions, trimmed
185 g (6½ oz) can of tuna
40 g (1½ oz) butter or margarine
1.25 ml (¼ level tsp) chilli powder
15 ml (1 level tbsp) plain flour
1 garlic clove, skinned and crushed
400 g (14 oz) can of chopped tomatoes
50 ml (2 fl oz) white wine
5 ml (1 level tsp) sugar
about 225 g (8 oz) frozen shelled mussels, thawed
freshly grated Parmesan cheese, to serve

1 Cook the pasta in a large saucepan of boiling salted water for 5–8 minutes or until just tender.
2 Meanwhile, slice the spring onions into 5 cm (2 inch) lengths, discarding coarse green leaves. Drain and flake the tuna.
3 Heat the butter or margarine in a medium saucepan, add the spring onions and fry until just beginning to colour. Stir in the chilli, flour and garlic, and cook, stirring, for 1–2 minutes.
4 Mix in the chopped tomatoes with the wine, sugar and salt and pepper to taste. Bring to the boil, then carefully stir in the tuna and mussels. Heat through for a few minutes. Taste and adjust the seasoning.
5 To serve, drain the pasta thoroughly and put in a warmed serving bowl. Gently spoon the sauce over the pasta and top with grated Parmesan.

505 Calories per serving

NOT SUITABLE FOR FREEZING

Pasta with Smoked Trout, Peppers and Almonds

Serves 4–6

3 large red peppers
400 g (14 oz) dried pasta shapes, such as bows or shells
salt and pepper
225 g (8 oz) smoked trout fillets
60 ml (4 tbsp) olive oil
45 ml (3 level tbsp) chopped fresh dill
75 g (3 oz) flaked almonds, toasted
40 g (1½ oz) butter
fresh dill, to garnish

1 Halve and deseed the peppers. Place the pepper halves, cut sides down, on the grill rack and grill for about 20 minutes or until the skins are charred. Allow to cool slightly, then, holding the pepper halves over a bowl to catch any juices, remove the skins. Cut the peppers into thin strips.
2 Cook the pasta in a large saucepan of boiling salted water for 10–12 minutes or until just tender.
3 Meanwhile, flake the smoked trout fillets.
4 Heat the oil in a large frying pan. Place the pepper strips and any reserved juices in the pan and heat through for 1 minute. Stir in the chopped dill, almonds and flaked trout, and heat for 1 minute. Remove from the heat and stir in the butter; this will prevent any further cooking. Season with salt and pepper.
5 To serve, drain the pasta thoroughly. Add to the smoked trout mixture and toss lightly to mix. Serve garnished with dill.

785–525 Calories per serving

NOT SUITABLE FOR FREEZING

Pasta with Tuna and Olive Sauce

Serves 4

50 g (2 oz) can of anchovy fillets
milk for soaking
15 ml (1 tbsp) olive oil
1 onion, skinned and chopped
1 garlic clove, skinned and crushed
5 ml (1 level tsp) dried marjoram
400 g (14 oz) can of chopped tomatoes
350 g (12 oz) dried pasta shapes
salt and pepper
200 g (7 oz) can of tuna steaks in brine, drained
and flaked
50 g (2 oz) black or green olives
30 ml (2 tbsp) dry white wine
fresh marjoram, to garnish (optional)
freshly grated Parmesan cheese, to serve

1 To remove much of the salt from the anchovies, drain well and place in a bowl. Cover with milk and soak for 20 minutes. Drain, pat dry with absorbent kitchen paper and chop.
2 To make the sauce, heat the oil in a saucepan, add the onion and cook gently for 5 minutes. Add the garlic, dried marjoram and tomatoes. Bring to the boil and simmer for 15 minutes or until slightly thickened, stirring occasionally.
3 Meanwhile, cook the pasta in a large saucepan of boiling salted water for 10–12 minutes or until just tender.
4 Add the tuna, anchovies and olives to the sauce. Return to the boil, stirring, then reduce the heat and simmer for 2–3 minutes. Stir in the wine, and season with pepper. Drain the pasta and serve hot with the sauce spooned over. Garnish with fresh marjoram, if wished, and top with grated Parmesan.

COOK'S TIP

There is no need to add any salt to the sauce as the anchovies contain enough residual salt to season the dish.

495 Calories per serving

NOT SUITABLE FOR FREEZING

Creamy Tuna and Pasta

Serves 4

225 g (8 oz) dried pasta shapes, such as
spirals or bows
salt and pepper
25 g (1 oz) butter
150 ml (5 fl oz) soured cream
5 ml (1 tsp) anchovy essence
30 ml (2 tbsp) malt vinegar
200 g (7 oz) can of tuna steaks in brine, drained
and flaked
4 eggs, hard-boiled, shelled and finely chopped
60 ml (4 level tbsp) chopped fresh parsley

1 Cook the pasta in a large saucepan of boiling salted water for 10–12 minutes or until just tender. Drain well.
2 Melt the butter in a deep frying pan and toss in the pasta. Stir in the soured cream, anchovy essence and vinegar.
3 Add the tuna and eggs to the pan with the parsley. Season well with salt and pepper, and warm through over a low heat, stirring occasionally. Serve immediately.

500 Calories per serving

NOT SUITABLE FOR FREEZING

SAUCES FOR PASTA

VEGETARIAN

PASTA WITH LEEKS AND FROMAGE FRAIS

SERVES 2

45 ml (3 tbsp) olive oil
225 g (8 oz) leeks, trimmed, sliced and washed
150 ml (5 fl oz) vegetable stock
225–275 g (8–10 oz) dried pasta
salt and pepper
300 ml (10 fl oz) fromage frais
15 ml (1 tbsp) horseradish relish
chopped fresh parsley, to garnish

1 Heat the oil in a saucepan, add the leeks and cook over a low heat for 4–5 minutes or until the leeks begin to soften. Add the stock and bring to the boil, then reduce the heat, cover and simmer for 15–20 minutes or until the leeks are very soft.
2 Meanwhile, cook the pasta in a large saucepan of boiling salted water for 10–12 minutes or until just tender.

3 Stir the fromage frais and horseradish into the leek mixture. Season with salt and pepper, and heat gently, without boiling, stirring all the time.
4 Drain the pasta and transfer to a warmed serving bowl. Pour the sauce over the pasta and serve, sprinkled with parsley.

895 Calories per serving

NOT SUITABLE FOR FREEZING

Pasta with Leeks and Fromage Frais (above)

Classic Tomato Sauce

Serves 4

15 ml (1 tbsp) olive oil
75 g (3 oz) onion, skinned and chopped
75 g (3 oz) celery, trimmed and chopped
75 g (3 oz) carrot, peeled and chopped
1 garlic clove, skinned and crushed
two 400 g (14 oz) cans of chopped tomatoes
30 ml (2 level tbsp) tomato purée
150 ml (5 fl oz) vegetable stock
100 ml (4 fl oz) dry red wine
salt and pepper
450 g (1 lb) dried pasta shapes, tagliatelle or spaghetti
50 g (2 oz) sun-dried tomatoes in olive oil (drained weight), finely chopped
freshly grated Parmesan cheese, to serve

1 Heat the olive oil in a large saucepan. Add the vegetables and garlic. Cook, stirring continuously, for 5 minutes or until beginning to soften but not colour.

2 Stir in the canned tomatoes, tomato purée, stock, wine and salt and pepper to taste. Simmer, covered, for about 30 minutes, stirring occasionally.

3 Meanwhile, cook the pasta in a large saucepan of boiling salted water for 10–12 minutes or until just tender.

4 In a blender or food processor, purée the sauce until smooth.

5 Return the sauce to the saucepan, add the sun-dried tomatoes, taste and adjust the seasoning. Reheat gently.

6 Drain the pasta and tip it into a warmed serving bowl. Top with Parmesan and serve at once.

495 Calories per serving

SUITABLE FOR FREEZING

VARIATIONS

CHILLI TOMATO SAUCE

Add 1 small, finely chopped red chilli in step 1.

MUSHROOM AND PARSLEY SAUCE

Add 125 g (4 oz) wiped and thinly sliced brown cap mushrooms and 30 ml (2 level tbsp) chopped fresh parsley when reheating the sauce.

Sweet Tomato Sauce

Serves 4

30 ml (2 tbsp) olive oil
125 g (4 oz) onion, skinned and finely chopped
1 garlic clove, skinned and crushed
175 g (6 oz) green pepper, deseeded and roughly chopped
two 400 g (14 oz) cans of tomatoes
1.25 ml (¼ level tsp) mild chilli powder
10 ml (2 level tsp) sugar
5 ml (1 level tsp) ready-made English mustard
5 ml (1 tsp) lemon juice
450 g (1 lb) dried pasta shapes or spaghetti
salt and pepper
30 ml (2 level tbsp) chopped fresh parsley

1 Heat the olive oil in a large saucepan, add the onion and garlic, and fry for about 5 minutes or until soft and golden. Stir in the green pepper and cook, stirring, for 2–3 minutes.

2 In a blender or processor, purée all the remaining ingredients, except the pasta and the parsley.

3 Stir the puréed tomato mix into the onion and pepper mixture. Bring to the boil, then simmer gently for about 30 minutes, uncovered, until the mixture becomes slightly thickened.

4 Meanwhile, cook the pasta in a large saucepan of boiling salted water for 10–12 minutes or until just tender. Drain well.

5 When the sauce is ready, season with salt and pepper and stir in the parsley. Serve at once, poured over the hot pasta.

515 Calories per serving

SUITABLE FOR FREEZING AFTER STEP 4

LENTIL AND TOMATO SAUCE

SERVES 3–4

30 ml (2 tbsp) olive oil
225 g (8 oz) onion, skinned and chopped
1 garlic clove, skinned and chopped
125 g (4 oz) red lentils, rinsed and drained
150 ml (5 fl oz) vegetable stock
400 g (14 oz) can of chopped tomatoes
150 g (5 oz) mushrooms, wiped and quartered
1 green pepper, deseeded and sliced
salt and pepper
350–450 g (12 oz–1 lb) dried pasta shapes
grated Gruyère cheese, to serve

1 Heat the oil in a saucepan, add the onions and garlic, and fry for 2–3 minutes or until soft.
2 Cook the lentils in a saucepan of rapidly boiling water for 10 minutes, then drain and add to the onion and garlic mixture. Stir until the lentils are completely coated in oil.
3 Add the stock, tomatoes, mushrooms, green pepper and salt and pepper to taste. Bring to the boil, then reduce the heat, cover and simmer for 30 minutes or until the lentils are soft.
4 Meanwhile, cook the pasta in a large saucepan of boiling salted water for 10–12 minutes or until just tender. Drain well and tip into a warmed serving bowl. Pour the sauce over the hot pasta, sprinkle with Gruyère cheese and serve.

795-595 Calories per serving

SUITABLE FOR FREEZING AFTER STEP 3

PENNE WITH TOMATO AND CHILLI

SERVES 4

30 ml (2 tbsp) olive oil
2 celery sticks, trimmed and finely chopped
1 small carrot, peeled and finely chopped
1 medium onion, skinned and finely chopped
1–2 garlic cloves, skinned and crushed
30 ml (2 level tbsp) tomato purée
5 ml (1 level tsp) dried herbes de Provence
1–2 fresh red chillies, deseeded and chopped
two 400 g (14 oz) cans of chopped tomatoes
150 ml (5 fl oz) dry red wine or vegetable stock
a handful of fresh parsley (including some stalks), chopped
salt and pepper
450 g (1 lb) dried penne (pasta 'quills')

1 Heat the oil in a large heavy-based saucepan. Add the celery, carrot, onion and garlic and cook over a high heat for 2–3 minutes, stirring all the time. Lower the heat and continue cooking for about 5 minutes or until the vegetables are beginning to soften without browning.
2 Add the tomato purée, dried herbs and chillies, increase the heat and fry for 1–2 minutes. Add the tomatoes, red wine or stock and half the parsley. Season with salt and pepper and bring to the boil, then lower the heat, cover and simmer for 45 minutes.
3 Cook the pasta in a large saucepan of boiling salted water for 10–12 minutes or until just tender.
4 While the pasta is cooking, remove the lid from the sauce, increase the heat and cook vigorously until it is reduced and thickened. Add the remaining parsley, taste and adjust the seasoning.
5 Drain the pasta and tip it into the sauce. Toss together to mix and serve immediately.

530 Calories per serving

SAUCE SUITABLE FOR FREEZING

SPAGHETTI WITH RATATOUILLE SAUCE

SERVES 4

1 aubergine, diced
salt and pepper
1 onion, skinned and finely chopped
1 garlic clove, skinned and crushed
1 red pepper, deseeded and cut into thin strips
3 medium courgettes, trimmed and thinly sliced
350 g (12 oz) tomatoes, skinned and finely sliced
10 ml (2 level tsp) chopped fresh basil
450 g (1 lb) dried wholewheat spaghetti
fresh basil, to garnish
freshly grated Parmesan cheese, to serve

1 Spread out the aubergine on a plate and sprinkle with salt. Leave for 20 minutes to draw out the bitter juices.

2 Tip the aubergine into a sieve and rinse under cold running water. Drain and put into a large, heavy-based saucepan with the onion, garlic, red pepper, courgettes, tomatoes, basil and salt and pepper to taste.

3 Cover and cook over moderate heat for 30 minutes, shaking the pan and stirring the vegetables frequently to encourage the juices to flow.

4 Meanwhile, cook the spaghetti in a large saucepan of boiling salted water for 10–12 minutes or until just tender. Drain well.

5 Place the spaghetti in a warmed serving dish. Taste and adjust the seasoning of the ratatouille sauce, then pour it over the spaghetti. Garnish with basil and serve immediately, with the Parmesan cheese handed separately.

410 Calories per serving

SUITABLE FOR FREEZING AFTER STEP 3

Spaghetti with Ratatouille Sauce (above)

Vegetarian Spaghetti Bolognese

Serves 8

30 ml (2 tbsp) olive oil
1 celery stick, trimmed and finely chopped
2 carrots, peeled and finely chopped
1 onion, skinned and finely chopped
125 g (4 oz) mushrooms, wiped and finely chopped
2 garlic cloves, skinned and crushed
45 ml (3 level tbsp) tomato purée
two 400 g (14 oz) cans of chopped tomatoes
300 ml (½ pint) dry red wine
600 ml (1 pint) vegetable stock
1 bay leaf
1 bouquet garni
5 ml (1 tsp) yeast extract savoury spread
5 ml (1 level tsp) sugar
salt and pepper
freshly grated nutmeg, to taste
1 cinnamon stick
175 g (6 oz) soya mince (dried weight)
900 g (2 lb) dried spaghetti
45 ml (3 level tbsp) chopped fresh parsley

1 Heat the oil in a large, heavy-based saucepan, add the celery, carrots, onion, mushrooms and garlic, and fry for about 5 minutes or until softened.
2 Add the tomato purée and fry for 1 minute, then add all the remaining ingredients, except the pasta and parsley.
3 Bring to the boil, then reduce the heat, cover and simmer gently for 30–45 minutes or until the soya mince is very tender.
4 Meanwhile, cook the spaghetti in a large saucepan of boiling salted water for 10–12 minutes or until just tender. Drain well and tip into a warmed serving bowl.
5 Stir the parsley into the sauce and season with more salt, pepper and nutmeg, if necessary.

Remove the cinnamon stick, bay leaf and bouquet garni and pour over the hot pasta. Serve at once.

540 Calories per serving

SUITABLE FOR FREEZING AFTER STEP 3

VARIATION

To make a spicy version, add 1–2 chopped fresh green chillies instead of the bay leaf and bouquet garni.

Pasta with Mushroom and Hummus Sauce

Serves 2

30 ml (2 tbsp) olive oil
225 g (8 oz) button mushrooms, wiped and sliced
1 bunch of spring onions, trimmed and chopped
pinch of cumin seeds
225 g (8 oz) hummus
30 ml (2 tbsp) milk
225 g (8 oz) dried spaghetti or tortellini
salt and pepper

1 Heat the oil in a saucepan, add the vegetables and cumin seeds, and fry for 2–3 minutes, stirring constantly.
2 Add the hummus and milk. Cover and simmer for 5–10 minutes.
3 Meanwhile, cook the pasta in a large saucepan of boiling salted water for 10–12 minutes or until just tender. Drain well.
4 Stir the pasta into the sauce and season with salt and pepper.

770 Calories per serving

NOT SUITABLE FOR FREEZING

*P*ASTA PRIMAVERA

SERVES 4–6

175 g (6 oz) fine asparagus

salt and pepper

125 g (4 oz) sugar-snap peas, topped and tailed

225 g (8 oz) carrots, preferably whole baby ones

50 g (2 oz) butter

1 small onion, skinned and chopped

1 red pepper, deseeded and diced

2 celery sticks, trimmed and diced

2 courgettes, trimmed and diced

6–8 spring onions, trimmed and sliced

400 g (14 oz) dried tagliatelle or pappardelle noodles

300 ml (10 fl oz) double cream

60 ml (4 level tbsp) freshly grated Parmesan cheese

20 ml (4 level tsp) snipped fresh chives

20 ml (4 level tsp) chopped fresh chervil

20 ml (4 level tsp) chopped fresh dill

1 Halve the asparagus and cook in boiling salted water for 3–4 minutes. Add the sugar-snaps after 2 minutes so that both are cooked until just tender. Drain, refresh under cold running water, then drain again and set aside.

2 If the carrots are baby ones, scrub them and leave them whole; if not cut them into matchsticks.

3 Melt the butter in a large frying pan, add the onion, and fry over a medium heat for 7–8 minutes or until soft and golden. Add the red pepper and celery, and cook for 5 minutes. Stir in the courgettes, carrots and spring onions, and cook for 12–15 minutes, stirring frequently, until the vegetables are tender and beginning to colour.

4 Meanwhile, cook the pasta in a large saucepan of boiling salted water for 10–12 minutes or until just tender.

5 Stir the cream into the vegetables and bring to a gentle boil. Allow to bubble, stirring frequently, for a few minutes, until it reduces by about one-third. Stir in the asparagus and sugar snaps. Add the Parmesan and heat through gently. Season to taste.

6 Drain the pasta and transfer to a warmed serving bowl. Toss the pasta into the sauce and sprinkle with the herbs. Serve at once.

950–635 Calories per serving

NOT SUITABLE FOR FREEZING

VARIATION

At other times of year, substitute different vegetables and herbs for the spring/summer selection suggested here.

SPAGHETTI WITH GARLIC

SERVES 6

450 g (1 lb) dried spaghetti
salt and pepper
75 ml (5 tbsp) olive oil
2 garlic cloves, skinned and crushed
1 chilli, deseeded and chopped
30 ml (2 level tbsp) chopped fresh parsley,
coriander or basil (optional)

1 Cook the spaghetti in a large saucepan of boiling salted water for 10–12 minutes or until just tender.

2 Meanwhile, heat the oil in a heavy-based saucepan, add the garlic and chilli and fry for 3–4 minutes, stirring occasionally. Don't let the garlic and chilli become too brown or the oil will taste bitter. Remove from the heat and set aside until the pasta is cooked.

3 Drain the pasta thoroughly. Reheat the oil over a very high heat for 1 minute, then pour over the pasta with the herbs, if using. Season with salt and pepper and serve immediately.

375 Calories per serving

NOT SUITABLE FOR FREEZING

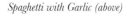

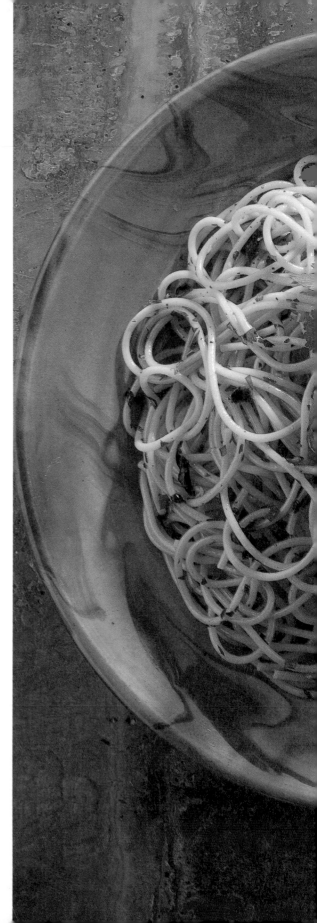

Spaghetti with Garlic (above)

Pasta with Caper Sauce and Grilled Cheese

Serves 4–6

2 red peppers, halved and deseeded
90 ml (6 tbsp) olive oil
2 onions, skinned and chopped
2 garlic cloves, skinned and crushed
45 ml (3 level tbsp) chopped fresh parsley
50 g (2 oz) capers, drained
salt and pepper
400 g (14 oz) dried penne (pasta 'quills'),
rigatoni or tagliatelle
225 g (8 oz) halloumi cheese

1 Preheat the grill to hot. Grill the red pepper halves, skin side up, for 10–15 minutes or until the skin is blistered and blackened. Cover and leave to cool slightly, then peel. Cut into strips and set aside.

2 Heat 75 ml (5 tbsp) olive oil in a large frying pan. Add the onions and cook over a medium heat, stirring frequently, for 7–8 minutes or until soft. Stir in the garlic and continue cooking for a further 2–3 minutes or until the onion is golden brown. Stir in the chopped parsley.

3 Rinse the capers thoroughly to remove the vinegar, and roughly chop them. Add to the onion mixture. Season lightly with salt and pepper (remember that halloumi cheese is very salty).

4 Cook the pasta in a large saucepan of boiling salted water for 10–12 minutes or until just tender.

5 Meanwhile, cut the halloumi into 1 cm ($\frac{1}{2}$ inch) slices. Place these in a baking tin large enough to take them in one layer. Add the remaining 15 ml (1 tbsp) olive oil and plenty of pepper. Grill, turning occasionally, for 4–5 minutes or until the cheese is golden on both sides. Remove from the tin and dice.

6 Drain the pasta and return it to the saucepan. Add the caper sauce and the reserved pepper strips. Toss well to mix in the sauce. Transfer to a warmed serving bowl or plates and sprinkle with the grilled cheese. Serve at once.

755–505 Calories per serving

NOT SUITABLE FOR FREEZING

Fresh Tagliatelle with Fennel

Serves 6

1 large fennel bulb, trimmed and chopped
salt and pepper
75 g (3 oz) butter
2 large garlic cloves, skinned and crushed
5 ml (1 level tsp) grated lemon rind
300 ml (10 fl oz) double cream
45 ml (3 level tbsp) chopped fresh fennel leaves
pinch of freshly grated nutmeg
juice of 1 lemon
350 g (12 oz) fresh plain tagliatelle
350 g (12 oz) fresh spinach tagliatelle
75 g (3 oz) Parmesan cheese, freshly grated

1 Blanch the fennel in a saucepan of boiling salted water for 2 minutes. Drain well.

2 Melt half the butter in a pan, add the garlic, and fry gently for 2–3 minutes, stirring. Add the blanched fennel and lemon rind and cook gently for 3 minutes.

3 Add the remaining butter and the cream and

bring the mixture almost to the boil. Stir in the fennel leaves, and add salt, pepper, nutmeg and lemon juice to taste.

4 Cook the tagliatelle in a large saucepan of boiling salted water for 3–5 minutes or until just tender. Drain well and tip into a warmed serving bowl.

5 Spoon half the fennel sauce over the pasta. Add 25 g (1 oz) of the Parmesan cheese, and toss until the sauce coats the pasta. Serve with the remaining sauce and Parmesan cheese handed separately.

COOK'S TIP

The subtle aniseed flavour of fresh fennel goes perfectly with pasta in this creamy sauce flavoured with garlic and lemon.

550 Calories per serving

NOT SUITABLE FOR FREEZING

2 Drain the artichokes well, leave to cool slightly, then purée in a blender or food processor until smooth.

3 Add the soured cream to the artichoke purée and season to taste.

4 Cook the pasta in a large saucepan of boiling salted water for 3–5 minutes or until just tender. Drain well, then spread in the base of four lightly greased, shallow flameproof dishes.

5 Arrange the eggs over the noodles and spoon the artichoke sauce evenly over each dish.

6 Place under a hot grill for 3–4 minutes or until golden. Serve immediately.

COOK'S TIP

Jerusalem artichokes have a pleasant and distinctive flavour and texture. The small, brown, knobbly tubers are tricky to peel, so bear this in mind when shopping and do not choose any that are too small or lumpy.

585 Calories per serving

NOT SUITABLE FOR FREEZING

EGG AND ARTICHOKE WITH FRESH NOODLES

SERVES 4

450 g (1 lb) Jerusalem artichokes, peeled and cut into large chunks

150 ml (5 fl oz) soured cream

salt and pepper

450 g (1 lb) fresh tagliatelle, or other noodles

6 eggs, hard-boiled, shelled and quartered

1 Put the artichokes into a medium saucepan and cover with water. Bring to the boil, then reduce the heat and simmer for 15–20 minutes or until they are very tender.

SPINACH-STUFFED PASTA SHELLS

SERVES 2

10 large dried pasta shells
salt and pepper
450 g (1 lb) fresh spinach, trimmed, or
225 g (8 oz) frozen spinach
1-2 garlic cloves, skinned and crushed
125 g (4 oz) low-fat soft cheese
freshly grated nutmeg, to taste
150 ml (5 fl oz) natural low-fat yogurt
15 ml (1 level tbsp) tomato purée
finely grated rind and juice of ½ lemon

1 Cook the pasta in a large saucepan of boiling salted water for 10–12 minutes or until just tender.
2 Meanwhile, wash the fresh spinach, if using, in several changes of water and chop roughly. Cook with just the water clinging to the leaves for 3–4 minutes or until just wilted. If using frozen spinach, cook for about 10 minutes or until thawed. Drain the spinach and chop finely.
3 Mix the spinach with the garlic and cheese, and season generously with nutmeg and salt and pepper. Leave to cool.
4 Drain the pasta, rinse under cold running water, then drain again. Stuff the pasta shells with the spinach mixture.
5 Mix the yogurt, tomato purée and lemon rind and juice together and season with salt and pepper. Pour over the stuffed shells. Serve cold.

600 Calories per serving

NOT SUITABLE FOR FREEZING

NEAPOLITAN TORTELLONI

SERVES 4

10 ml (2 tsp) sunflower oil
2 garlic cloves, skinned and finely chopped
225 ml (8 fl oz) passata or other sieved tomatoes
2.5 ml (½ level tsp) dried oregano
salt and pepper
450 g (1 lb) fresh spinach-stuffed
tortelloni
15 g (½ oz) Parmesan cheese, freshly grated

1 Heat the oil in a non-stick saucepan, add the garlic and cook gently until beginning to change colour. Add the passata and oregano, and season with salt and pepper. Bring to the boil, turn off the heat and cover. Keep warm while cooking the pasta.
2 Cook the tortelloni in a large saucepan of boiling salted water for 10–12 minutes or until just tender. Drain well.
3 Divide the tortelloni between four warmed soup plates, pour the sauce over and sprinkle with the Parmesan cheese.

380 Calories per serving

NOT SUITABLE FOR FREEZING

*F*RESH TAGLIATELLE WITH LEEK AND ROQUEFORT SAUCE

SERVES 4

75 g (3 oz) butter

1 garlic clove, skinned and crushed

450 g (1 lb) leeks, trimmed, sliced and washed

150 g (5 oz) Roquefort cheese, roughly chopped

30 ml (2 level tbsp) chopped fresh chervil or
10 ml (2 level tsp) dried chervil

700 g (1½ lb) fresh tagliatelle

salt and pepper

5 ml (1 tsp) olive oil

150 ml (5 fl oz) whipping cream

15-30 ml (1–2 level tbsp) freshly grated
Parmesan cheese

chervil sprigs, to garnish

1 Melt 50 g (2 oz) of the butter in a medium saucepan, add the garlic and leeks and fry for 2–3 minutes or until softened.

2 Stir in the Roquefort cheese and chervil. Cook for 2–3 minutes or until the cheese has melted, stirring constantly.

3 Meanwhile, add the tagliatelle to a large saucepan of boiling salted water, with the olive oil added, and cook for 3–4 minutes. Drain and return to the clean pan. Add the remaining butter, toss well and season with pepper.

4 Pour the cream into the cheese sauce, whisking vigorously. Cook, stirring, for a few minutes or until thick.

5 Serve the tagliatelle on warmed individual serving plates with the sauce poured over. Sprinkle with Parmesan cheese and garnish with chervil sprigs.

1005 Calories per serving

NOT SUITABLE FOR FREEZING

SAUCES FOR PASTA

LEAN AND HEALTHY

SERVES 4

175 g (6 oz) dried pasta shapes
salt and pepper
40 g (1½ oz) very low-fat spread, such as Flora
Extra Light
25 g (1 oz) plain flour
450 ml (¾ pint) semi-skimmed milk
40 g (1½ oz) Parmesan cheese, freshly grated

1 Cook the pasta in a large saucepan of boiling salted water for 10–12 minutes or until just tender.
2 Meanwhile, melt the spread in a small saucepan over a low heat, stir in the flour and cook for a few seconds, stirring.
3 Remove from the heat and gradually add the milk, whisking until smooth. Slowly bring to the boil, stirring, then simmer gently for 4–5 minutes, whisking again if necessary.
4 Off the heat, stir in the cheese and season to taste.
5 Drain the pasta and tip into a warmed serving bowl. Pour over the sauce, toss well and serve.

130 Calories per serving of sauce

280 Calories per serving with 40 g (1½ oz) pasta

NOT SUITABLE FOR FREEZING

VARIATIONS

WHOLEGRAIN MUSTARD AND TARRAGON SAUCE

(130 Calories per serving of sauce)
At step 3, stir in 10 ml (2 level tsp) wholegrain mustard and 20 ml (4 level tsp) chopped fresh tarragon or 2.5 ml (½ level tsp) dried tarragon.

RICH CHEESE SAUCE

For an extra-rich cheese sauce, you can add 50 g (2 oz) grated Edam cheese to the recipe for only an extra 40 Calories per serving, or stir in 50 g (2 oz) grated Gruyère for an extra 50 Calories.

COOK'S TIP

Heat low-fat spread gently as it burns easily. Don't boil the sauce after adding cheese as it may curdle.

*R*ICH TOMATO SAUCE

SERVES 4

15 ml (1 tbsp) olive oil from jar of sun-dried tomatoes
75 g (3 oz) onion, skinned and roughly chopped
75 g (3 oz) carrot, peeled and roughly chopped
75 g (3 oz) celery, trimmed and roughly chopped
1 garlic clove, skinned and crushed
125 g (4 oz) sun-dried tomatoes in olive oil, drained and finely chopped
two 400 g (14 oz) cans of chopped tomatoes
150 ml (5 fl oz) stock
100 ml (4 fl oz) dry white wine
salt and pepper
175 g (6 oz) dried pasta shapes

1 Heat the olive oil in a large saucepan, add the onion, carrot, celery and garlic, and cook, stirring, for about 5 minutes or until they begin to soften.
2 Stir in the tomatoes, stock and wine, and season with salt and pepper. Simmer, covered, for about 20 minutes, stirring occasionally.
3 Meanwhile, cook the pasta in a large saucepan of boiling salted water for 10–12 minutes or until just tender.
4 When the sauce is cooked, leave it to cool slightly, then purée in a blender or food processor until smooth. Return to the saucepan, taste and adjust the seasoning, and reheat gently.
5 Drain the pasta well and tip it into a warmed serving bowl. Pour over the sauce and serve at once.

120 Calories per serving of sauce

270 Calories per serving with 40 g (1½ oz) pasta

SUITABLE FOR FREEZING AT THE END OF STEP 4 WHEN COOL

*B*EEF AND SPLIT PEA SAUCE

SERVES 4

10 ml (2 tsp) olive oil
225 g (8 oz) onion, skinned and chopped
1 garlic clove, skinned and crushed
225 g (8 oz) lean minced beef
125 g (4 oz) split yellow peas
450 ml (¾ pint) beef stock
400 g (14 oz) can of chopped tomatoes
30 ml (2 level tbsp) tomato purée
30 ml (2 tbsp) Worcestershire sauce
salt and pepper
125 g (4 oz) dried spaghetti or small pasta shapes

1 Heat the oil in a saucepan, add the onion and garlic and fry for 3–4 minutes or until softened.
2 Add the beef and split peas, and cook for 2–3 minutes, stirring occasionally. Mix in the rest of the ingredients, except the pasta. Season well with salt and pepper.
3 Bring to the boil, then reduce the heat, cover and simmer for 45–50 minutes or until tender.
4 Meanwhile, cook the pasta in a large saucepan of boiling salted water for 10–12 minutes or until just tender. Drain well and tip into a warmed serving bowl. Pour over the sauce and serve.

250 Calories per serving of sauce

350 Calories per serving with 25 g (1 oz) pasta

SAUCE SUITABLE FOR FREEZING

Vegetable, Pasta and Lentil Pot

Serves 4

450 g (1 lb) onion, carrot and celery

350 g (12 oz) mixed green vegetables, such as broccoli, courgettes and French beans

15 ml (1 tbsp) olive oil

50 g (2 oz) smoked streaky bacon or chorizo, derinded and roughly chopped

2 garlic cloves, skinned and crushed

75 g (3 oz) green lentils

1.4 litres (2½ pints) ham or chicken stock

75 g (3 oz) dried tortelloni

salt and pepper

chopped fresh parsley, to serve

1 Prepare as necessary and finely chop the onion, carrot and celery. Cut the green vegetables into bite-sized pieces.

2 Heat the oil in a large saucepan and add the onion, carrot, celery, bacon and garlic. Cook over a moderate heat until beginning to brown.

3 Stir in the lentils and the stock. Bring to the boil, then reduce the heat, cover and simmer for 10 minutes.

4 Stir in the tortelloni, re-cover and simmer for a further 10 minutes. Add the remaining vegetables, re-cover and simmer for 5 minutes or until tender.

5 Taste and adjust the seasoning, sprinkle with chopped fresh parsley and serve.

255 Calories per serving

NOT SUITABLE FOR FREEZING

Crunchy Vegetable Pasta

Serves 4

175 g (6 oz) dried pasta shapes

salt and pepper

15 ml (1 tbsp) olive oil

125 g (4 oz) onion, skinned and finely chopped

1 garlic clove, skinned and crushed

1.25 ml (¼ level tsp) mild chilli powder

1 red pepper, deseeded and diced

225 g (8 oz) tomatoes, diced

225 g (8 oz) courgettes, trimmed and diced

350 ml (12 fl oz) tomato juice

15 ml (1 tbsp) red wine vinegar

30 ml (2 level tbsp) chopped fresh parsley

20 ml (4 level tsp) freshly grated Parmesan cheese

1 Cook the pasta in a large saucepan of boiling salted water for 10–12 minutes or until just tender.

2 Meanwhile, heat the oil in a non-stick frying pan, add the onion and garlic, and cook for about 3 minutes or until beginning to soften. Stir in the chilli powder and cook for a further minute.

3 Add the red pepper, tomatoes and courgettes to the frying pan and cook over a medium heat for about 5 minutes or until hot but still crunchy. Stir in the tomato juice and vinegar with plenty of seasoning. Bring to the boil, then reduce the heat and simmer for 2-3 minutes or until piping hot.

4 Drain the pasta well and tip into a warmed serving bowl. Spoon the sauce over the pasta and serve immediately, sprinkled with chopped parsley and Parmesan cheese.

260 Calories per serving

SAUCE SUITABLE FOR FREEZING

Crunchy Vegetable Pasta (above)

Pasta in Sweet Pepper Sauce

SERVES 4

15 ml (1 tbsp) olive oil
450 g (1 lb) red peppers, deseeded and finely chopped
225 g (8 oz) onion, skinned and finely chopped
1 garlic clove, skinned and crushed
400 g (14 oz) can of chopped tomatoes
600 ml (1 pint) vegetable stock
salt and pepper
50 g (2 oz) salami, roughly chopped
225 g (8 oz) dried pasta
25 g (1 oz) Parmesan cheese, freshly grated
60 ml (4 level tbsp) chopped fresh basil

1 Heat the oil in a frying pan, add the vegetables and garlic, and fry for 5–7 minutes or until beginning to soften, stirring frequently.
2 Stir in the tomatoes and stock, cover and simmer gently for 25–30 minutes or until the peppers are soft. Uncover and boil until most of the liquid has evaporated.
3 Season the sauce with salt and pepper, add the salami and heat through gently.
4 Meanwhile, cook the pasta in a large saucepan of boiling salted water for 10–12 minutes or until just tender. Drain well and tip into a warmed serving bowl. Pour over the sauce and sprinkle with Parmesan cheese and basil. Serve at once.

360 Calories per serving

SUITABLE FOR FREEZING AFTER STEP 2

Pasta with Leeks and Lemon Mayonnaise

SERVES 4

60 ml (4 level tbsp) reduced-calorie mayonnaise
150 ml (5 fl oz) very low-fat fromage frais
grated rind and juice of 1 lemon
1 garlic clove, skinned and crushed
salt and pepper
175 g (6 oz) dried pasta shapes
15 ml (1 tbsp) olive oil
700 g (1½ lb) trimmed leeks, sliced and washed
225 g (8 oz) brown-cap mushrooms, wiped and sliced
snipped fresh chives and finely grated lemon rind, to garnish

1 Mix together the mayonnaise, fromage frais, lemon rind and 15 ml (1 tbsp) lemon juice. Add the garlic and plenty of seasoning.
2 Cook the pasta in a large saucepan of boiling salted water for 10–12 minutes or until just tender. Drain well.
3 Meanwhile, heat the oil in a non-stick saucepan, add the leeks and mushrooms, and fry for 5–10 minutes or until golden brown and just softened. Season well.
4 Spoon the leeks and mushrooms over the hot pasta. Serve immediately with the lemon mayonnaise, and garnished with chives and lemon rind.

315 Calories per serving

NOT SUITABLE FOR FREEZING

Roast vegetable and pasta salad

SERVES 4

4 red peppers, deseeded and cut into
bite-sized pieces

255 g (8 oz) courgettes, trimmed and cut into
bite-sized pieces

225 g (8 oz) aubergine, trimmed and cut into
bite-sized pieces

2 celery sticks, trimmed and cut into
bite-sized pieces

4 whole garlic cloves, skinned

30 ml (2 tbsp) olive oil

salt and pepper

225 g (8 oz) tomatoes, halved

125 g (4 oz) dried pasta shapes, such as
penne ('quills')

125 g (4 oz) feta cheese, crumbled or cut into
bite-sized pieces

10 ml (2 tsp) balsamic vinegar

chopped fresh parsley, to garnish

1 Place all the vegetables, except the tomatoes, in a roasting tin with the whole garlic cloves, olive oil, and salt and pepper to taste. Mix well.

2 Cook the vegetables in the oven at 230°C (450°F) mark 8 for 40–50 minutes or until tender and well charred, adding the tomatoes for the last 20 minutes of cooking time.

3 About 15 minutes before the vegetables are ready, cook the pasta in a large saucepan of boiling salted water for 10–12 minutes or until just tender. Drain well.

4 Toss the pasta into the cooked vegetables with the feta cheese, balsamic vinegar and plenty of seasoning. Serve the salad immediately, garnished with chopped fresh parsley.

305 Calories per serving

NOT SUITABLE FOR FREEZING

Mixed mushroom pasta

SERVES 4

15 g (½ oz) dried porcini mushrooms

225 g (8 oz) dried spaghetti

salt and pepper

30 ml (2 tbsp) olive oil

1 small onion, skinned and finely chopped

1 garlic clove, skinned and crushed

225 g (8 oz) button or brown-cap mushrooms,
wiped and finely chopped

50 ml (2 fl oz) fromage frais

fresh rosemary sprigs, to garnish (optional)

1 Soak the dried porcini mushrooms in 300 ml (½ pint) warm water for about 20 minutes. Remove with a slotted spoon and reserve the soaking liquid. Chop the soaked mushrooms.

2 Cook the pasta in a large saucepan of boiling salted water for 10–12 minutes or until just tender.

3 Meanwhile, heat the oil in a frying pan, add the onion and garlic, and fry for 3–4 minutes or until just beginning to soften. Add all the mushrooms and fry for 2–3 minutes, stirring constantly. Add the reserved soaking liquid and allow to bubble over a high heat for about 5 minutes or until reduced by half. Off the heat, stir in the fromage frais and season with salt and pepper.

4 Drain the pasta well and stir it into the mushroom sauce. Garnish with fresh rosemary sprigs, if wished, and serve immediately.

305 Calories per serving

NOT SUITABLE FOR FREEZING

PASTA WITH MEATBALLS, SHALLOTS AND OLIVES

SERVES 4

275 g (10 oz) shallots or small onions, skinned
30 ml (2 tbsp) olive oil
225 g (8 oz) lean minced beef
30 ml (2 level tbsp) chopped fresh parsley
salt and pepper
25 g (1 oz) pitted black olives
30 ml (2 level tbsp) chopped fresh chives
30 ml (2 level tbsp) pesto sauce
125 g (4 oz) dried pasta noodles, such as tagliatelle or fettucine

1 Chop 50 g (2 oz) of the shallots or onions.
2 Heat 15 ml (1 tbsp) of the oil in a frying pan, add the chopped shallot or onion and fry for about 10 minutes or until golden. Cool, then mix into the mince with the parsley and salt and pepper to taste.
3 Shape the mince mixture into eight small patties. Fry in a non-stick pan for 5–7 minutes on each side or until cooked through.
4 Meanwhile, thinly slice the remaining shallots or onions and cook in the remaining oil in a covered pan for 8–10 minutes or until soft and golden. Stir in the olives, chives and pesto, warm through and adjust the seasoning.
5 Cook the pasta in a large saucepan of boiling salted water for 10–12 minutes or until just tender. Drain well.
6 Toss the noodles with the shallot/onion mixture and serve immediately, accompanied by the meatballs.

335 Calories per serving

NOT SUITABLE FOR FREEZING

CRESPOLINE

SERVES 4

225 g (8 oz) fresh spinach or 125 g (4 oz) frozen
leaf spinach, thawed
175 g (6 oz) ricotta cheese
pinch of freshly grated nutmeg
1 garlic clove, skinned and crushed
salt and pepper
8 dried pasta cannelloni tubes, about 75 g (3 oz)
total weight
300 ml (½ pint) Rich Tomato Sauce (see page 57)
1 quantity Parmesan Sauce (see page 56)

1 Wash the fresh spinach, if using, and put it in a large saucepan with just the water clinging to the leaves. Cover tightly and cook for 3–4 minutes or until wilted. Drain well, cool and chop roughly. (There's no need to cook frozen spinach.)
2 Mix the spinach with the ricotta, nutmeg, garlic and salt and pepper to taste. Fill the pasta tubes with this mixture.
3 Pour the tomato sauce into an ovenproof dish and place the cannelloni on top in a single layer. Cover with the Parmesan sauce. (There is a lot, but it soaks into the pasta.) Leave to stand for 30 minutes before cooking.
4 Cook in the oven at 190°C (375°F) mark 5 for 30–40 minutes or until piping hot and golden brown. Serve at once.

330 Calories per serving

NOT SUITABLE FOR FREEZING

COOK'S TIP

If the cheese sauce gets too hot it may separate slightly around the edges, but it is still delicious. Most cannelloni does not need any pre-cooking, but check the packet instructions first.

Crespoline (above)

CHILLI PORK WITH NOODLES

SERVES 4

350 g (12 oz) pork fillet (tenderloin)
225 g (8 oz) yellow pepper, halved and deseeded
225 g (8 oz) broccoli
30 ml (2 tbsp) olive oil
125 g (4 oz) onion, skinned and roughly chopped
2.5 ml (½ level tsp) mild chilli powder or a few drops of Tabasco sauce
5 ml (1 level tsp) dried oregano or dried mixed herbs
50 g (2 oz) dried pasta noodles, such as tagliatelle or fettucine
30 ml (2 tbsp) sherry or medium white wine
450 ml (¾ pint) beef stock
15 ml (I level tbsp) hoisin or soy sauce
pepper

1 Trim the pork of any excess fat and cut into thin slices. Cut the pepper into similar-sized pieces. Thinly slice the broccoli stalks and divide the remainder into small florets.

2 Heat the oil in a large non-stick frying pan or wok, add the pork and cook, stirring, for 2–3 minutes or until well browned.

3 Remove the pork from the pan with a slotted spoon and drain on absorbent kitchen paper. Add all the vegetables to the pan with the chilli powder and herbs, and fry, stirring, for 1–2 minutes.

4 Mix in the pork with the pasta, sherry or wine, stock and hoisin or soy sauce. Bring to the boil, then reduce the heat, cover and simmer for about 10 minutes or until all the ingredients are tender. Adjust the seasoning, adding pepper as necessary.

285 Calories per serving

SUITABLE FOR FREEZING

BEEF PASTA GRATIN

SERVES 4

about 50 g (2 oz) large dried pasta shells
½ quantity Beef and Split Pea Sauce
(see page 57; make full quantity and freeze half)
1 quantity Parmesan Sauce (see page 56)
15 g (½ oz) freshly grated Parmesan cheese

1 Cook the pasta shells in a large saucepan of boiling salted water for 10–12 minutes or until just tender. Drain well.

2 Reheat the Beef and Split Pea Sauce and use to fill the cooked pasta shells. Place in a shallow flameproof dish.

3 Spoon the Parmesan Sauce over and sprinkle with freshly grated Parmesan. Place under a hot grill for 3–4 minutes or until golden. Serve immediately, with remaining sauces separately.

350 Calories per serving

NOT SUITABLE FOR FREEZING

Beef Pasta Gratin (above)

*B*ACON AND MUSHROOM CARBONARA

SERVES 4

175 g (6 oz) dried pasta shapes, such as penne ('quills'), shells, etc
salt and pepper
250 g (9 oz) jar of mixed mushrooms in oil
225 g (8 oz) onion, skinned and chopped
1 garlic clove, skinned and crushed
50 g (2 oz) smoked back bacon, chopped
3 eggs
60 ml (4 level tbsp) very low-fat fromage frais
60 ml (4 level tbsp) chopped fresh parsley
20 ml (4 level tsp) freshly grated Parmesan cheese
chopped fresh parsley, to garnish

1 Cook the pasta in a large saucepan of boiling salted water for 10–12 minutes or until just tender. Meanwhile, drain the mushrooms and reserve the oil. Heat 15 ml (1 tbsp) of the reserved oil in a frying pan, add the onion and garlic, and fry for about 5 minutes or until soft.
2 Add the mushrooms and bacon to the pan, and cook for 3–4 minutes.
3 Whisk together the eggs, fromage frais and seasoning. Drain the pasta and stir it into the hot mushroom and bacon mixture. Off the heat, pour in the egg mixture and stir well – the heat of the pasta will lightly cook the egg. Add the parsley and season. Serve sprinkled with Parmesan cheese and chopped fresh parsley.

COOK'S TIP

Jars of mixed mushrooms in oil are available from most supermarkets and delicatessens.

350 Calories per serving

NOT SUITABLE FOR FREEZING

*S*PINACH AND HAM MACARONI

SERVES 4

150 g (5 oz) dried macaroni
salt and pepper
200 g (7 oz) fresh spinach
75 g (3 oz) thinly sliced smoked ham
1 quantity Parmesan Sauce (see page 56)
150 ml (5 fl oz) semi-skimmed milk
10 ml (2 level tsp) wholegrain mustard
15 g (½ oz) freshly grated Parmesan cheese
25 g (1 oz) fresh breadcrumbs

1 Cook the pasta in a large saucepan of boiling salted water for 10–12 minutes or until just tender. Drain well.
2 Shred the spinach and ham. Heat the Parmesan Sauce in a saucepan, then add the milk. Mix together the spinach, ham, pasta, sauce, mustard and seasoning. Transfer to a shallow, ovenproof dish and sprinkle with the cheese and breadcrumbs.
3 Cook in the oven at 190°C (375°F) mark 5 for 30–35 minutes or until piping hot. Serve immediately.

335 Calories per serving

SUITABLE FOR FREEZING

Gingered Chicken and Noodles

SERVES 4

15 ml (1 tbsp) olive oil

1 bunch of spring onions, trimmed and sliced

2.5 cm (1 inch) piece of fresh root ginger, peeled and grated

1 garlic clove, skinned and crushed

275 g (10 oz) skinless chicken breast fillet, cut into bite-sized pieces

30 ml (2 level tbsp) mild curry paste or 15 ml (1 level tbsp) Thai hot curry paste

300 ml (½ pint) coconut milk (see Cook's Tip)

about 300 ml (½ pint) chicken stock

salt and pepper

125 g (4 oz) dried pasta noodles, such as tagliatelle or fettucine

10 ml (2 tsp) lemon or lime juice

1 Heat the oil in a large non-stick frying pan, add the spring onions, ginger and garlic, and fry until just beginning to soften. Add the chicken pieces and curry paste and cook for a further 3–4 minutes or until golden brown.

2 Stir in the coconut milk, stock and salt and pepper to taste. Bring to the boil, then add the pasta, cover and simmer for 10–12 minutes or until the pasta is just tender, stirring occasionally. Add a little more stock if the mixture becomes too dry. Add the lemon or lime juice, season to taste and serve immediately, stirring well to mix.

COOK'S TIP

Use canned coconut milk or roughly chop a 50 g (2 oz) block of creamed coconut and make up to 300 ml (½ pint) with boiling water. Stir well to mix.

310 Calories per serving

NOT SUITABLE FOR FREEZING

Pasta with Chicken Liver Sauce

SERVES 4

225 g (8 oz) chicken livers, thawed if frozen

15 ml (1 tbsp) oil

125 g (4 oz) onion, skinned and chopped into bite-sized pieces

1 garlic clove, skinned and crushed

75 g (3 oz) lean smoked back bacon or salami, cut into bite-sized pieces

50 ml (2 fl oz) dry white wine

400 g (14 oz) can of chopped tomatoes

15 ml (1 level tbsp) tomato purée

300 ml (½ pint) chicken stock

salt and pepper

175 g (6 oz) dried pasta shapes

chopped fresh basil and a little freshly grated Parmesan cheese, to serve

1 Trim the livers and cut into bite-sized pieces.

2 Heat the oil in a large, non-stick frying pan, add the livers, and fry until golden brown. Remove from the pan.

3 Add the onion, garlic and bacon to the pan, and fry for 3–4 minutes.

4 Stir in the remaining ingredients, except the livers and pasta, with plenty of seasoning. Cover and simmer for 15 minutes.

5 Meanwhile, cook the pasta in boiling salted water for 10–12 minutes or until just tender.

6 Stir the chicken livers into the bacon and tomato mixture, and simmer for a further 2–3 minutes or until the livers are cooked.

7 Drain the pasta well and tip it into a warmed serving bowl. Taste the sauce and adjust the seasoning, if necessary, then stir in some chopped basil and pour over the hot pasta. Sprinkle lightly with Parmesan cheese.

350 Calories per serving with 40 g (1½ oz) pasta

NOT SUITABLE FOR FREEZING

PASTA WITH PAN-FRIED SALMON

SERVES 4

275 g (10 oz) skinned salmon fillet
15 ml (1 tbsp) olive oil
125 g (4 oz) dried pasta shapes
salt and pepper
15 ml (1 level tbsp) plain white flour
300 ml (½ pint) skimmed milk
30 ml (2 level tbsp) chopped fresh parsley
30 ml (2 level tbsp) capers, drained
50 g (2 oz) can of anchovy fillets, drained
1 garlic clove, skinned and crushed
5 ml (1 level tsp) Dijon mustard
15 ml (1 tbsp) lemon juice
flat-leafed parsley, to garnish

1 Cut the salmon into thick slices. Heat the oil in a non-stick frying pan, add the salmon and fry for 5–7 minutes, turning once.

2 Meanwhile, cook the pasta in a large saucepan of boiling salted water for 10–12 minutes or until just tender.

3 Mix the flour to a paste with a little milk. Place in a saucepan with the remaining milk, 150 ml (5 fl oz) water and the next six ingredients. Bring slowly to the boil, stirring, then reduce the heat and simmer for 2–3 minutes. Season (don't use much salt as anchovies are salty).

4 Serve the salmon on a bed of pasta. Spoon the sauce over and garnish with parsley.

COOK'S TIP

If you find anchovies salty, soak them in milk for about 20 minutes, then drain before using.

340 Calories per serving

NOT SUITABLE FOR FREEZING

SEAFOOD SPAGHETTI WITH PEPPER AND ALMOND SAUCE

SERVES 4

1 small red pepper, about 150 g (5 oz)
1 fresh red chilli
50 g (2 oz) toasted, blanched almonds
2–3 garlic cloves, skinned and crushed
30 ml (2 tbsp) red wine vinegar
350 ml (12 fl oz) tomato juice
60 ml (4 level tbsp) chopped fresh parsley
salt and pepper
125 g (4 oz) dried spaghetti
450 g (1 lb) mixed prepared and cooked seafood, such as prawns, mussels and squid
chopped fresh chilli, to garnish

1 Place the pepper and chilli under the grill and cook, turning occasionally, until the skins blacken. Cool slightly, then pull off the skins. Halve the pepper and chilli, discard the seeds, then put the flesh into the bowl of a food processor.

2 Add the nuts, garlic, vinegar, tomato juice, half the parsley and seasoning. Blend until almost smooth, then transfer to a saucepan.

3 Cook the pasta in a large saucepan of boiling salted water for 10–12 minutes or until just tender. Drain and toss in the rest of the fresh parsley. Season and cover.

4 Meanwhile, gently heat the sauce until it simmers, then add the seafood. Simmer for 3–4 minutes or until heated through, stirring frequently. Adjust the seasoning and serve immediately over the hot spaghetti. Garnish with chilli.

300 Calories per serving

NOT SUITABLE FOR FREEZING

Seafood Spaghetti with Pepper and Almond Sauce (above)

*S*AUCES FOR PASTA

QUICK AND EASY

*T*OMATO SAUCE

SERVES 4

30 ml (2 tbsp) olive oil
1 small onion, skinned and finely chopped
30 ml (2 level tbsp) tomato purée
5 ml (1 level tsp) mild paprika
two 400 g (14 oz) cans of chopped tomatoes
large pinch of dried oregano
300 ml (½ pint) dry red wine or vegetable stock
large pinch of sugar
salt and pepper
450 g (1 lb) dried pasta

1 Heat the oil in a saucepan, add the onion, and fry for 5–10 minutes or until soft. Add the tomato purée and paprika, and fry for 2–3 minutes. Add the tomatoes, oregano, wine or stock, and sugar.
2 Season the sauce with salt and pepper and bring to the boil, then reduce the heat and simmer, uncovered, for about 20 minutes or until the sauce is slightly reduced.
3 Meanwhile, cook the pasta in a large saucepan of boiling salted water for 10–12 minutes or until just tender. Drain well and tip into a warmed serving bowl. Spoon the sauce on top and serve at once.

165 Calories per serving

SUITABLE FOR FREEZING AT END OF STEP 2

VARIATION

Add 1–2 chopped fresh chillies and a little chopped fresh coriander.

70

*H*AZELNUT AND CORIANDER PESTO

SERVES 4–6

75 g (3 oz) shelled hazelnuts, with skins on
1 large bunch of fresh coriander, about 125 g (4 oz), stalks removed
2–3 garlic cloves, skinned and crushed
finely grated rind and juice of ½ lemon
about 150 ml (5 fl oz) olive oil
salt and pepper
450 g (1 lb) dried pasta

1 Toast the hazelnuts under a hot grill. Tip them on to a clean tea towel and rub off the loose skins. Toast again under the grill until golden on all sides. Leave to cool, then tip into a blender or food processor.
2 Put the coriander leaves into the blender or food processor with the hazelnuts. Add the garlic and the lemon rind and juice, and process until finely chopped.
3 With the machine still running, gradually add the oil in a thin, steady stream, as if making mayonnaise, until you have a fairly thick, sauce-like consistency. Season with pepper and a little salt.
4 Cook the pasta in a large saucepan of boiling salted water for 10–12 minutes or until just tender. Drain well and tip into warmed serving bowls. Top with spoonfuls of the pesto and toss well before serving.

COOK'S TIPS

This makes a vibrant green pesto with a pungent smell and a strong flavour. Serve it separately for guests to mix to taste with their individual plates of steaming pasta. It can be stored for up to 2 weeks in a screw-topped jar in the refrigerator.

465–310 Calories per serving

NOT SUITABLE FOR FREEZING

*P*ESTO

SERVES 4–6

50 g (2 oz) basil leaves (weighed without stalks)
2 garlic cloves, skinned
30 ml (2 tbsp) pine kernels
salt and pepper
100 ml (4 fl oz) olive oil
50 g (2 oz) Parmesan cheese, freshly grated
450 g (1 lb) dried pasta

1 Put the basil, garlic, pine kernels, salt, pepper and olive oil in a mortar and pound with a pestle, or place in a blender or food processor and blend at high speed until very creamy.
2 Transfer the mixture to a bowl, fold in the cheese and mix thoroughly.
3 Cook the pasta in a large saucepan of boiling salted water for 10–12 minutes or until just tender. Drain well and tip into warmed serving bowls. Top with spoonfuls of pesto and toss well before serving.

COOK'S TIP

This classic pesto sauce can be served with small dried pasta shapes or spaghetti or noodles. Stored in a screw-topped jar in the refrigerator, the sauce will keep for up to 2 weeks.

75 Calories per 15 ml (1 tbsp) sauce

NOT SUITABLE FOR FREEZING

Overleaf: Tomato Sauce (page 70)

Walnut and Basil Sauce for Pasta

Serves 4

2 large garlic cloves, skinned

40 g (1½ oz) fresh basil leaves (a large bunch)

50 g (2 oz) Parmesan cheese, freshly grated

1 small tomato, skinned, deseeded and roughly chopped

60 ml (4 tbsp) olive oil

salt and pepper

350 g (12 oz) fresh or 225 g (8 oz) dried pasta

45 ml (3 tbsp) single cream

50 g (2 oz) walnut pieces, roughly chopped

fresh basil sprigs and freshly grated Parmesan cheese, to serve

1 Put the garlic, basil, Parmesan cheese and tomato in a blender or food processor and work to a smooth paste.

2 With the machine still running, gradually add the olive oil, drop by drop, as if making mayonnaise. Season the mixture with salt and pepper, and store, covered, in the refrigerator until required.

3 Cook the pasta in a large saucepan of boiling salted water for 2–4 minutes (for fresh pasta) or 10–12 minutes (for dried pasta) or until just tender. Drain well, then toss in a warmed serving bowl with the cream, basil sauce and walnuts. Serve at once with fresh basil sprigs and grated Parmesan cheese.

480 Calories per serving

NOT SUITABLE FOR FREEZING

Walnut and Bacon Sauce

Serves 4

350 g (12 oz) fresh or 225 g (8 oz) dried pasta

salt and pepper

50 ml (2 fl oz) olive oil

275 g (10 oz) smoked back bacon, derinded and chopped

1 garlic clove, skinned and crushed

75 g (3 oz) walnut pieces, chopped

450 g (1 lb) tomatoes, skinned and chopped

60 ml (4 level tbsp) chopped fresh parsley

grated rind of 1 lemon

225 g (8 oz) soft cheese, such as goats' cheese or full-fat cheese with garlic and herbs, to serve (optional)

1 Cook the pasta in a large saucepan of boiling salted water for 2–4 minutes (for fresh pasta) or for 10–12 minutes (for dried pasta) or until just tender.

2 Meanwhile, heat the oil in a large frying pan, add the bacon, garlic and walnuts, and fry together until golden, stirring occasionally.

3 Stir in the tomatoes, parsley and grated lemon rind. Heat, stirring, for 1–2 minutes, or until piping hot. Season with black pepper.

4 Drain the pasta well and tip it into a warmed serving bowl. Top with the sauce and toss well together. Serve immediately, topping each portion with pieces of soft cheese, if you like.

775 Calories per serving

NOT SUITABLE FOR FREEZING

VARIATION

Fry 1–2 shallots, cut into segments, with the bacon, garlic and walnuts. Serve the pasta garnished with sprigs of parsley.

*N*OODLES IN WALNUT SAUCE

SERVES 4

125 g (4 oz) walnut pieces
75 g (3 oz) butter, softened
1 small garlic clove, skinned and roughly chopped
30 ml (2 level tbsp) plain flour
300 ml (½ pint) milk
275 g (10 oz) fresh spinach tagliatelle
salt and pepper
125 g (4 oz) Cheddar cheese, grated
pinch of freshly grated nutmeg

1 In a blender or food processor, mix together the walnuts, 50 g (2 oz) of the butter and the garlic. Place in a bowl.

2 Put the remaining butter in the blender or food processor. Add the flour and milk, and work until evenly mixed.

3 Place the mixture in a saucepan and bring slowly to the boil, stirring. Reduce the heat and simmer for 6 minutes.

4 Meanwhile, cook the tagliatelle in a large saucepan of boiling salted water for 2–4 minutes or until just tender. Drain thoroughly, then return to the pan. Add the nut butter and heat through gently, stirring.

5 Divide the pasta mixture between four large, individual gratin-type dishes. Season the white sauce with salt and pepper, then use to coat the pasta.

6 Scatter the grated cheese on top, sprinkle with the nutmeg, then grill for 5–10 minutes or until brown and bubbling. Serve immediately.

705 Calories per serving

NOT SUITABLE FOR FREEZING

*P*ASTA WITH PECAN AND PARSLEY SAUCE

SERVES 3

50 g (2 oz) pecan nuts, shelled
25 g (1 oz) parsley sprigs
45 ml (3 level tbsp) freshly grated Parmesan cheese
100 ml (4 fl oz) olive oil
60 ml (4 tbsp) curd or low-fat soft cheese
salt and pepper
350 g (12 oz) dried tricolour pasta twists
extra freshly grated Parmesan cheese, to serve

1 Put the nuts and parsley in a blender or food processor and blend until finely chopped.

2 Blend in the Parmesan cheese, then, with the machine still running, gradually add the oil, a little at a time, as if making mayonnaise. Transfer to a saucepan and stir in the curd or soft cheese. Season with salt and pepper.

3 Cook the pasta in a large saucepan of boiling salted water for 10–12 minutes or until just tender. Drain well and return to the rinsed-out saucepan.

4 Heat the sauce gently, without boiling, then stir into the pasta and serve with extra Parmesan.

875 Calories per serving

NOT SUITABLE FOR FREEZING

PASTA WITH GARLIC AND OIL SAUCE

SERVES 4

350 g (12 oz) fresh or 225 g (8 oz) dried pasta
salt and pepper
120 ml (8 tbsp) olive oil
2 garlic cloves, skinned and finely chopped

1 Cook the pasta in a large saucepan of boiling salted water for 2–4 minutes (for fresh pasta) or 10–12 minutes (for dried pasta) or until just tender.

2 Meanwhile, put the oil, garlic and seasoning in a small saucepan and fry very gently, stirring all the time, for 2–3 minutes or until the garlic is golden.

3 Drain the pasta well and tip it into a warmed serving bowl. Pour over the garlic sauce and toss together before serving.

600 Calories per serving

NOT SUITABLE FOR FREEZING

NOODLES AND COURGETTES

SERVES 3

2 ripe tomatoes, skinned and chopped
15 ml (1 level tbsp) chopped fresh coriander
30 ml (2 level tbsp) chopped fresh parsley
grated rind and juice of 1 lemon
30 ml (2 tbsp) olive oil
1 garlic clove, skinned and crushed
salt and pepper
125 g (4 oz) green beans, topped, tailed and halved
175 g (6 oz) courgettes, trimmed and sliced
350 g (12 oz) fresh pasta
sprig of fresh coriander, to garnish

1 Mix the tomatoes with the coriander, parsley, lemon rind and juice, oil, garlic and seasoning.

2 Steam the beans and courgettes for 5 minutes or until just tender. Drain.

3 Cook the pasta in a large saucepan of boiling salted water for 2–4 minutes or until just tender. Drain well and tip into a large warmed serving bowl.

4 Place the tomato mixture in the pan and heat through gently. Add the steamed vegetables and mix them together lightly. Spoon over the pasta, garnish with coriander and serve immediately.

465 Calories per serving

NOT SUITABLE FOR FREEZING

Noodles and Courgettes (above)

CREAM SAUCE

SERVES 4

350 g (12 oz) fresh or 225 g (8 oz) dried pasta
salt and pepper
25 g (1 oz) butter
300 ml (10 fl oz) double cream
25 g (1 oz) Parmesan cheese, freshly grated
extra freshly grated Parmesan cheese, to serve

1 Cook the pasta in a large saucepan of boiling salted water for 2–4 minutes (for fresh pasta) or 10–12 minutes (for dried pasta) or until just tender.
2 Meanwhile, melt the butter in a saucepan, pour in the cream and bring to the boil. Cook for 2–3 minutes, stirring constantly, until slightly thickened. Season with salt and pepper and stir in the Parmesan cheese.
3 Drain the pasta well and tip it into a warmed serving bowl. Top with the cream sauce and toss well together before serving with extra Parmesan cheese.

740 Calories per serving

NOT SUITABLE FOR FREEZING

PASTA WITH WATERCRESS AND GOATS' CHEESE

SERVES 4

350 g (12 oz) dried pasta shapes, such as spirals, bows or shells
salt and pepper
25 g (1 oz) fresh soft goats' cheese
45 ml (3 tbsp) single cream
45 ml (3 tbsp) roughly chopped watercress

1 Cook the pasta in a large saucepan of boiling salted water for 10–12 minutes or until just tender.
2 Meanwhile, beat together the cheese and cream.
3 Drain the pasta. Toss in the watercress and cheese mixture. Season and serve immediately.

COOK'S TIP

The heat of the freshly cooked pasta wilts the watercress and melts the goats' cheese mixture to form a sauce.

335 Calories per serving

NOT SUITABLE FOR FREEZING

SPAGHETTI WITH BLUE CHEESE SAUCE

SERVES 4

350 g (12 oz) dried spaghetti
salt and pepper
300 ml (10 fl oz) single cream
125 g (4 oz) Danish Blue cheese, roughly chopped

1 Cook the spaghetti in a large saucepan of boiling salted water for 10–12 minutes or until just tender.
2 Heat the cream in a saucepan over a very low heat and add the cheese. Heat until the cheese has melted, then season with salt and pepper.
3 Drain the pasta and place in a warmed serving dish. Pour the sauce over the pasta and serve.

555 Calories per serving

NOT SUITABLE FOR FREEZING

TAGLIATELLE WITH SAGE, PIMENTOS AND GARLIC

SERVES 4–6

60 ml (4 tbsp) olive oil
1 small onion, skinned and finely chopped
2 garlic cloves, skinned and crushed
400 g (14 oz) dried green and white tagliatelle
salt and pepper
400 g (14 oz) can of pimentos in brine, drained
30 ml (2 level tbsp) chopped fresh sage
150 ml (5 fl oz) extra-thick double cream
75 ml (5 level tbsp) freshly grated
Parmesan cheese
sage sprigs, to garnish

1 Heat the oil in a frying pan, add the onion and garlic, and cook over a medium heat for 5 minutes or until soft but not brown.
2 Cook the pasta in a large saucepan of boiling salted water for 10-12 minutes or until just tender.
3 Meanwhile, rinse the canned pimentos, then drain well and cut into fairly small dice. Add to the frying pan with the chopped sage and continue cooking for 5 minutes. Stir in the cream and bring to a simmer, then stir in all but 15 ml (1 level tbsp) of the Parmesan cheese. Season with salt and pepper.
4 Drain the pasta well and put it in a warmed serving bowl. Add the sauce to the pasta and toss well to mix. Serve sprinkled with the remaining grated Parmesan and garnished with sage.

775-520 Calories per serving

NOT SUITABLE FOR FREEZING

PASTA WITH ASPARAGUS AND PARMESAN

SERVES 4–6

400 g (14 oz) thin asparagus
50 g (2 oz) butter
1 onion, skinned and finely chopped
75 ml (3 fl oz) dry white wine
400 g (14 oz) dried pasta shapes, such as spirals
or penne ('quills')
salt and pepper
300 ml (10 fl oz) extra-thick double cream
50 g (2 oz) Parmesan cheese, freshly grated

1 Cut the asparagus into 5 cm (2 inch) lengths and blanch in boiling water for 2 minutes or until tender. Drain, reserving 75 ml (5 tbsp) of the cooking water, and set aside.
2 Melt the butter in a heavy-based frying pan, add the onion and cook over a medium-high heat for about 5 minutes or until softened and beginning to colour. Stir in the asparagus and cook for 1 minute. Pour in the reserved cooking water and the white wine. Cook over a high heat until almost all the liquid has evaporated.
3 Cook the pasta in a large saucepan of boiling salted water for 10–12 minutes or until just tender.
4 Meanwhile, add the cream to the sauce and stir well. Heat until bubbling. Stir in half of the grated Parmesan and season to taste with salt and pepper.
5 Drain the pasta well and transfer to a warmed serving bowl. Pour the cream sauce over it and toss well before serving sprinkled with the remaining Parmesan and pepper to taste.

875–585 Calories per serving

NOT SUITABLE FOR FREEZING

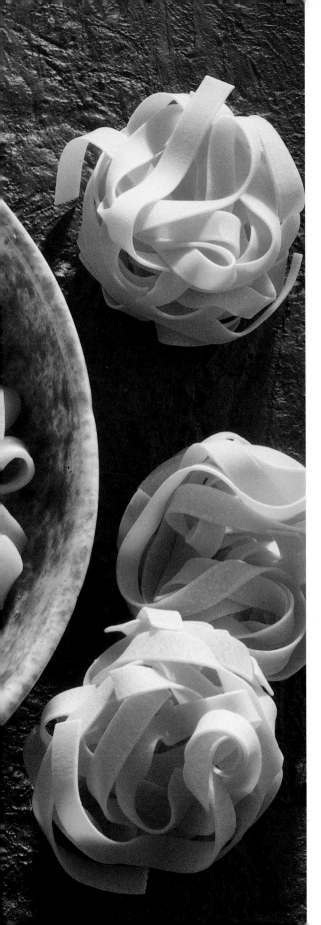

*F*ETTUCINE WITH GORGONZOLA SAUCE

SERVES 4–6

25 g (1 oz) butter
175 g (6 oz) Gorgonzola cheese
150 ml (5 fl oz) double cream
30 ml (2 tbsp) dry white wine
30 ml (2 level tbsp) chopped fresh basil
salt and pepper
450 g (1 lb) dried fettucine

1 Melt the butter in a saucepan, crumble in the Gorgonzola cheese and stir over a gentle heat for 2–3 minutes or until melted. Pour in the cream and wine, whisking vigorously. Mix in the basil and season with salt and pepper, then remove from the heat.
2 Meanwhile, cook the fettucine in a large saucepan of boiling salted water for 10–12 minutes or until just tender. Drain thoroughly.
3 Gently reheat the Gorgonzola sauce, whisking vigorously all the time. Turn the pasta into warmed serving bowls and pour over the sauce. Serve at once.

COOK'S TIP

For extra flavour, sprinkle with freshly shredded basil and coarsely ground pepper to serve.

785–525 Calories per serving

NOT SUITABLE FOR FREEZING

───────────────── ℞ ─────────────────

Fettucine with Gorgonzola Sauce (above)

TAGLIATELLE IN CURD CHEESE AND HERB SAUCE

Serves 2

15 g (½ oz) butter

1 garlic clove, skinned and crushed

50 g (2 oz) mushrooms, wiped and sliced

5 ml (1 level tsp) chopped fresh sage or 2.5 ml (½ level tsp) dried sage

50 g (2 oz) cooked ham, diced

125 g (4 oz) dried tagliatelle

salt

50 g (2 oz) medium-fat curd cheese

1 Melt the butter in a frying pan, add the garlic, mushrooms and sage, and fry for 2 minutes, then stir in the ham.

2 Cook the tagliatelle in a large saucepan of boiling salted water for 10–12 minutes or until just tender.

3 Add the cheese to the mushroom mixture and stir until melted.

4 Drain the tagliatelle and tip it into a warmed serving bowl. Pour over the sauce and serve immediately.

350 Calories per serving

NOT SUITABLE FOR FREEZING

LEEK, BACON AND CREAM CHEESE SAUCE

Serves 4

350 g (12 oz) dried pasta

salt and pepper

25 g (1 oz) butter or margarine

225 g (8 oz) mushrooms, wiped and thinly sliced

125 g (4 oz) leeks, trimmed, sliced and washed

125 g (4 oz) streaky bacon, derinded and roughly chopped

1 garlic clove, skinned and crushed

125 g (4 oz) low-fat soft cheese with garlic and herbs

30 ml (2 tbsp) milk or single cream

1 Cook the pasta in a large saucepan of boiling salted water for 10–12 minutes or until just tender.

2 Meanwhile, melt the butter or margarine in a medium saucepan, add the mushrooms, leeks, bacon and garlic, and fry for 3–4 minutes or until the leeks are tender but still retain some bite.

3 Reduce the heat and stir in the cheese and milk or cream until thoroughly mixed. Season with salt and pepper.

4 Drain the pasta and tip it into a warmed serving bowl. Spoon the leek mixture on top and serve at once.

455 Calories per serving

NOT SUITABLE FOR FREEZING

PASTA WITH PETITS POIS AND HAM IN CREAM SAUCE

SERVES 4

275–350 g (10–12 oz) dried tagliatelle
salt and pepper
125 g (4 oz) butter
1 large onion, skinned and sliced
125 g (4 oz) ham, cut into thin strips
125 g (4 oz) frozen petits pois, cooked
60 ml (4 tbsp) single cream
125 g (4 oz) Cheddar cheese, grated

1 Cook the tagliatelle in a large saucepan of boiling salted water for 10–12 minutes or until just tender.

2 Meanwhile, melt the butter in a pan, add the onion, and cook for about 3 minutes or until soft. Add the ham and peas and cook for a further 5 minutes.

3 Drain the tagliatelle and add to the pan. Stir well and add the cream and most of the cheese. Toss gently, season to taste and serve at once, sprinkled with the remaining cheese.

650 Calories per serving

NOT SUITABLE FOR FREEZING

TAGLIATELLE WITH GORGONZOLA AND SPINACH

SERVES 4–6

350 g (12 oz) young leaf spinach
225 g (8 oz) Gorgonzola cheese
75 ml (3 fl oz) milk
25 g (1 oz) butter
salt and pepper
400 g (14 oz) fresh tagliatelle

1 Wash the spinach thoroughly and remove any large stalks. Place in a saucepan with only the water clinging to the leaves, and cook, stirring, over a medium-high heat for 2–3 minutes or until wilted. Drain well in a colander, pressing out any excess liquid.

2 Cut the Gorgonzola into small pieces. Place in a clean pan with the milk and butter. Heat gently, stirring, until melted to a creamy sauce. Stir in the drained spinach. Season to taste with pepper (salt may not be necessary because the Gorgonzola is naturally quite salty).

3 Just before serving, cook the pasta in a large saucepan of boiling salted water for 2–4 minutes or until just tender.

4 Drain the pasta well and tip into a warmed serving bowl. Spoon over the sauce and toss well before serving.

630-420 Calories per serving

NOT SUITABLE FOR FREEZING

PENNE WITH OLIVES, ANCHOVIES AND CHILLI

SERVES 4–6

400 g (14 oz) dried pasta shapes, such as
penne ('quills')

salt and pepper

50 g (2 oz) can of anchovies in olive oil

2.5 ml (½ level tsp) dried chilli flakes

2 garlic cloves, skinned and crushed

30 ml (2 level tbsp) chopped fresh parsley

225 g (8 oz) mixed pitted black and green olives

60 ml (4 tbsp) olive oil

30-45 ml (2-3 level tbsp) freshly grated
Parmesan cheese

extra Parmesan cheese, to serve

1 Cook the pasta in a large saucepan of boiling salted water for 10–12 minutes or until just tender.
2 Meanwhile, put the anchovies, their oil, chilli flakes and garlic in a small pan. Cook over a fairly high heat for 2–3 minutes, stirring with a wooden spoon to break up the anchovies. Do not brown the garlic. Stir in the parsley and remove the pan from the heat.
3 Transfer the contents of the pan to a food processor and add the olives and olive oil. Process for a few seconds to give a coarse paste. Season with pepper.
4 Drain the pasta, return it to the saucepan and add the pounded olive mixture and the Parmesan cheese. Toss well to coat the pasta. Serve immediately, topped with extra Parmesan.

660–440 Calories per serving

NOT SUITABLE FOR FREEZING

VARIATION

Replace the anchovies with 50 g (2 oz) chopped sun-dried tomatoes in 15 ml (1 tbsp) of their oil, and cook as above.

FRESH TAGLIATELLE WITH SEAFOOD SAUCE

SERVES 6

30 ml (2 tbsp) grapeseed oil

1 small onion or 2 shallots, skinned and finely
chopped

1 garlic clove, skinned and crushed

two 225 g (8 oz) packets of ready-cooked
seafood cocktail

470 g (1 lb) jar of traditional-style pasta sauce

lemon juice, to taste

dry vermouth, to taste

salt and pepper

450 g (1 lb) fresh spinach tagliatelle or other
noodles

fresh parsley, to garnish

1 Heat the oil in a large frying pan, add the onion and garlic, and fry for 3–5 minutes or until just beginning to colour.
2 Add the mixed seafood and pasta sauce with a little lemon juice and vermouth to taste. Add salt and pepper to taste and heat gently.
3 Cook the pasta in a large saucepan of boiling salted water for 2–4 minutes or until just tender. Drain, then tip into a warmed serving bowl and add a splash of oil and some pepper. Toss and serve with the sauce, garnished with parsley.

COOK'S TIP

Use dried spinach tagliatelle, if preferred, and increase the cooking time to 10–12 minutes or until the pasta is just tender.

445 Calories per serving

NOT SUITABLE FOR FREEZING

Penne with Olives, Anchovies and Chilli (above)

84

*P*ASTA BAKES

*L*ASAGNE

SERVES 4–6

1 quantity Classic Bolognese Sauce
(see page 18)

about 350 g (12 oz) fresh lasagne, or 225 g (8 oz)
oven-ready dried lasagne (12–15 sheets)

45 ml (3 level tbsp) freshly grated Parmesan
cheese

FOR THE BECHAMEL SAUCE

900 ml (1½ pints) milk

3 slices of onion

3 bay leaves

18 peppercorns

3 blades of mace

40 g (1½ oz) butter or margarine

40 g (1½ oz) plain flour

salt and pepper

1 To make the béchamel sauce, pour the milk into a saucepan, add the onion, bay leaves, peppercorns and mace, and bring almost to the boil. Remove from the heat, cover and leave to infuse for 10–30 minutes. Strain.

2 Melt the butter or margarine in a saucepan. Remove from the heat and stir in the flour until evenly blended. Gradually pour on the warm milk, stirring well. Season lightly with salt and pepper. Bring to the boil, stirring constantly, and simmer for 2–3 minutes. Remove from the heat.

3 Spoon one third of the Bolognese Sauce into the base of a 2.3 litre (4 pint) ovenproof dish. Cover with a layer of lasagne, then spread over enough béchamel sauce to cover the pasta. Repeat these layers twice more, finishing with a layer of béchamel sauce to cover the lasagne completely.

4 Sprinkle the Parmesan cheese over the top and stand the dish on a baking sheet. Bake in the oven at 180°C (350°F) mark 4 for about 45 minutes or until well browned and bubbling. Leave to stand for about 5 minutes before serving.

COOK'S TIPS

Sheets of fresh lasagne are available in the chilled cabinet of most supermarkets. If using oven-ready dried lasagne, add a little extra stock or water to the sauce. You will find it easiest to use a large rectangular or square ovenproof dish.

465–310 Calories per serving

SUITABLE FOR FREEZING AFTER STEP 1

THREE-CHEESE LASAGNE

SERVES 8

400 g (14 oz) can of tomatoes
1 small onion, skinned and chopped
1 celery stick, trimmed and chopped
1 garlic clove, skinned and crushed
1 bay leaf
salt and pepper
450 g (1 lb) lean minced beef
1 egg, lightly beaten
50 g (2 oz) Parmesan cheese, freshly grated
75 g (3 oz) plain flour
60 ml (4 tbsp) olive or vegetable oil
75 g (3 oz) butter
750 ml (1¼ pints) milk
125 g (4 oz) mild cured ham, chopped
125 g (4 oz) Mozzarella cheese, grated
125 g (4 oz) Bel Paese cheese, cut into strips
150 ml (5 fl oz) single cream
400 g (14 oz) oven-ready dried lasagne

1 Place the tomatoes with their juice, the onion, celery, garlic and bay leaf in a small saucepan. Bring to the boil, then reduce the heat and simmer, uncovered, for 30 minutes, stirring occasionally.

2 Discard the bay leaf and rub the mixture through a sieve or purée in a blender. Season with salt and pepper.

3 Combine the beef, egg and half the Parmesan cheese. Season with salt and pepper and shape the mixture into 24 meatballs. Spread 15 g (½ oz) flour on a plate and season with salt and pepper. Roll the meatballs lightly in the flour.

4 Heat the oil in a frying pan, add the meatballs, and cook for about 5 minutes or until brown. Remove with a slotted spoon and drain.

5 Melt the butter in a pan, add the remaining 65g (2 oz) flour and cook for 1 minute, stirring. Remove from the heat and gradually stir in the milk.

6 Bring to the boil and cook, stirring, until the sauce thickens. Stir in the ham, Mozzarella, Bel Paese, cream and seasoning.

7 In a large, greased, ovenproof serving dish, layer up the lasagne, meatballs, tomato and white sauces, finishing with a layer of lasagne topped with white sauce.

8 Sprinkle the remaining Parmesan cheese over the top. Bake in the oven at 200°C (400°F) mark 6 for 20–25 minutes or until golden. Serve immediately.

730 Calories per serving

SUITABLE FOR FREEZING AFTER STEP 7

COOK'S TIP

Make sure you leave enough white sauce to make a substantial top layer. The lasagne sheets underneath should be completely covered, especially around the edges.

Pastitsio

SERVES 4

45 ml (3 tbsp) olive oil

125 g (4 oz) onion, skinned and finely chopped

2 garlic cloves, skinned and crushed

450 g (1 lb) lean minced lamb

7.5 ml (1½ level tsp) dried oregano

5 ml (1 level tsp) each dried thyme, ground cinnamon and ground cumin

2.5 ml (½ level tsp) each ground ginger and freshly grated nutmeg

1 bay leaf

150 ml (5 fl oz) dry white wine

400 g (14 oz) can of chopped tomatoes

salt and pepper

125 g (4 oz) dried pasta, such as macaroni or penne ('quills')

45 ml (3 level tbsp) chopped fresh coriander (optional)

25 g (1 oz) butter

25 g (1 oz) plain flour

450 ml (¾ pint) milk

50 g (2 oz) Parmesan cheese, freshly grated

2 eggs, beaten

1 Heat the oil in a saucepan, add the onion and garlic and cook gently for about 10 minutes, stirring occasionally, until the onions are soft.

2 Add the lamb and cook over a high heat for about 5 minutes, stirring, until evenly browned. Stir in the herbs, spices and bay leaf. Cook over a moderate heat for a further 5 minutes, stirring occasionally.

3 Mix in the wine, tomatoes and seasoning. Bring to the boil, then reduce the heat, cover and simmer for 30 minutes. Uncover and cook for about 15 minutes, stirring occasionally, until the sauce is thickened and well reduced. Taste and adjust the seasoning. Cool and skim off all fat.

4 Cook the pasta in a large saucepan of boiling salted water for 10–12 minutes or until just tender. Drain, then stir the pasta into the lamb with the chopped coriander, if using. Spoon into a shallow ovenproof dish.

5 Melt the butter in a saucepan. Stir in the flour, seasoning and milk. Bring to the boil, stirring, then simmer for 3–4 minutes or until thickened. Cool slightly. Off the heat, beat in the Parmesan cheese and eggs. Pour over the lamb mixture.

6 Cook in the oven at 190°C (375°F) mark 5 for 35–40 minutes or until golden brown and piping hot. Serve at once.

675 Calories per serving

SAUCE SUITABLE FOR FREEZING AT THE END OF STEP 3

Pastitsio (above)

LAMB AND WATERCRESS LASAGNE

SERVES 4–6

450 g (1 lb) minced lamb

2 large onions, skinned and finely chopped

2 bunches of watercress, trimmed and finely chopped

10 ml (2 level tsp) dried oregano

105 ml (7 level tbsp) plain flour

300 ml (½ pint) lamb or chicken stock

50 ml (2 fl oz) dry white wine

salt and pepper

25 g (1 oz) butter

600 ml (1 pint) milk

175 g (6 oz) Lancashire cheese, crumbled

225 g (8 oz) oven-ready lasagne verde

1 Put the lamb in a large saucepan and cook it in its own fat until well browned. Pour off excess fat. Add the onions to the pan and cook for 5 minutes, stirring occasionally. Add the watercress, oregano and 30 ml (2 tbsp) of the flour. Cook for 1–2 minutes, then gradually stir in the stock and wine and season with salt and pepper. Bring to the boil, then reduce the heat and simmer gently, uncovered, for 45 minutes, stirring occasionally.

2 Put the butter, remaining flour and milk in a saucepan. Heat, whisking continuously, until the sauce thickens, boils and is smooth. Simmer for 1–2 minutes. Remove the pan from the heat and stir in 125 g (4 oz) of the cheese. Stir until melted and season with salt and pepper.

3 Layer the mince mixture with the lasagne in a fairly deep ovenproof serving dish. Spoon over the cheese sauce.

4 Sprinkle with the remaining cheese and bake in the oven at 190°C (375°F) mark 5 for about 40 minutes or until browned. Serve hot.

755–505 Calories per serving

SUITABLE FOR FREEZING AT THE END OF STEP 3

LAMB LASAGNE GRATIN

SERVES 8

65 g (2½ oz) butter

700 g (1½ lb) mushrooms, wiped and chopped

15 ml (1 tbsp) vegetable oil

700 g (1½ lb) lean minced lamb

1 garlic clove, skinned and crushed

227 g (8 oz) can of tomatoes, drained

75 g (3 oz) plain flour

30 ml (2 level tbsp) chopped fresh herbs

150 ml (5 fl oz) dry white wine

salt and pepper

16 sheets of lasagne

900 ml (1½ pints) milk

125 g (4 oz) Cheddar cheese, grated

125 g (4 oz) Mozzarella cheese, chopped

1 Melt 25 g (1 oz) of the butter in a large saucepan, add the chopped mushrooms and cook over moderate heat for about 10 minutes or until they are soft.

2 Heat the oil in a large frying pan, add the lamb and cook until browned. Drain off all the fat.

3 Stir in the garlic, mushrooms, tomatoes, 30 ml (2 level tbsp) flour and the herbs. Cook for 1–2 minutes, then add the wine and season with salt and pepper. Bring to the boil, then reduce the heat and simmer for about 30 minutes, uncovered. Cool for 10 minutes.

4 Cook the lasagne sheets in a large saucepan of boiling salted water for about 12 minutes or until tender. Drain, rinse under cold running water and drain again. Spread the lamb mixture over the sheets of lasagne and roll up each sheet from one short side.

5 Cut each roll into three pieces. Pack tightly together, standing upright, in a large, deep, straight-sided flameproof serving dish.

6 Melt the remaining butter in a saucepan. Add the remaining flour and cook over a low heat, stirring, for 2 minutes. Gradually blend in the milk. Bring to the boil slowly, then simmer for 2–3 minutes, stirring. Season with salt and pepper.

7 Pour the sauce over the pasta and bake in the oven at 200°C (400°F) mark 6 for 40 minutes. Uncover, sprinkle with the cheese and grill until golden. Serve immediately.

640 Calories per serving

SUITABLE FOR FREEZING

BAKED STUFFED PASTA

SERVES 4–6

20 unpeeled garlic cloves
30 ml (2 tbsp) olive oil
15 g (½ oz) dried porcini mushrooms
3 shallots, skinned and finely chopped
450 g (1 lb) lean minced beef
150 ml (5 fl oz) red wine
30 ml (2 level tbsp) chopped fresh thyme
salt and pepper
about 12 sheets of lasagne
150 ml (5 fl oz) single cream
30 ml (2 level tbsp) sun-dried tomato paste
butter for greasing
75 g (3 oz) Gruyère or other strong cheese
herb sprigs, to garnish

1 Put the garlic in a roasting tin with 15 ml (1 tbsp) of the oil. Toss to coat the garlic in the oil and bake in the oven at 180°C (350°F) mark 4 for 25 minutes or until soft. Leave to cool.

2 Meanwhile, put the dried mushrooms in a small bowl and cover with 150 ml (5 fl oz) boiling water. Leave to soak for 20 minutes, then drain, reserving the liquor. Rinse the mushrooms, then chop finely.

3 Heat the remaining oil in a saucepan, add the shallots and cook for 5 minutes or until soft. Increase the heat, add the beef and cook until browned. Add the wine, mushrooms with their liquor and the thyme. Cook for 15–20 minutes or until most of the liquid has evaporated; the mixture should be quite moist.

4 Remove the papery skins from the garlic, then mash lightly to give a rough paste. Stir into the beef mixture, season and set aside.

5 Cook the lasagne sheets in a large saucepan of boiling salted water for about 12 minutes or until tender. Drain, rinse under cold running water and drain again.

6 Lay the lasagne sheets flat on a board or work surface. Spoon a little of the beef mixture along one long edge of each lasagne sheet, and roll up to enclose the filling. Cut the tubes in half.

7 In a bowl, mix together the cream and sun-dried tomato paste and season with pepper.

8 Butter a shallow baking dish and arrange a layer of the tubes in the base. Spoon half of the tomato cream over and sprinkle with half of the cheese. Arrange the remaining tubes on top and cover with the remaining tomato cream and cheese.

9 Cover the dish with foil and cook in the oven at 200°C (400°F) mark 6 for 10 minutes, then uncover and cook for a further 5–10 minutes or until lightly browned and hot. Serve at once, garnished with herbs.

815–545 Calories per serving

SUITABLE FOR FREEZING

CURRIED CHICKEN LASAGNE

SERVES 6

2 kg (4½ lb) oven-ready chicken
350 g (12 oz) dried lasagne
50 g (2 oz) butter or margarine
30 ml (2 level tbsp) plain flour
45 ml (3 level tbsp) medium curry powder
1.1 litres (2 pints) milk
salt and pepper
40 g (1½ oz) desiccated coconut
15 ml (1 level tbsp) fresh breadcrumbs

1 Skin the chicken and remove the flesh from the bones. Trim off the fat and cut the meat into 1 cm (½ inch) chunks.

2 Cook the lasagne in a large saucepan of boiling salted water for about 12 minutes or until just tender. (Even if you are using pre-cooked lasagne, you should still boil it for about 7 minutes.) Drain, rinse under cold running water, then drain on a clean cloth.

3 Melt the butter or margarine in a saucepan, stir in the flour and curry powder and cook for 1 minute, stirring. Remove from the heat and gradually stir in the milk. Bring to the boil slowly and continue to cook, stirring, until the sauce thickens. Simmer for 5 minutes, then season and add 25 g (1 oz) of the coconut.

4 Spoon some sauce over the base of a 2.3 litre (4 pint) shallow ovenproof dish. Arrange the lasagne and chicken in single layers, adding a little sauce to each layer. Finish with lasagne and pour the rest of the sauce over the top.

5 Sprinkle with the remaining coconut and breadcrumbs. Bake in the oven at 180°C (350°F) mark 4 for about 1 hour or until the top is brown.

640 Calories per serving

SUITABLE FOR FREEZING AT THE END OF STEP 4

CHICKEN PASTA ROLLS

SERVES 4

10 sheets of dried lasagne, about 150 g (5 oz) total weight
salt and pepper
275 g (10 oz) cooked, skinned roast chicken
2 bunches of watercress
150 g (5 oz) full-fat soft cheese with garlic and herbs
400 g (14 oz) crème fraîche
125 g (4 oz) cooked, thinly sliced ham
50 ml (2 fl oz) milk
a few saffron strands (optional)

1 Cook the lasagne in a large saucepan of boiling salted water for about 12 minutes or until just tender. Drain well, separate the sheets out on to a clean work surface and leave to cool.

2 Meanwhile, chop the chicken and finely chop the watercress. Mix together with the soft cheese and 30 ml (2 level tbsp) crème fraîche. Season to taste.

3 Cover the lasagne sheets with slices of ham. Spoon the chicken mixture along one short side of each sheet and roll up loosely. Cut the rolls into three and stand, cut side uppermost, in a small ovenproof dish.

4 Beat together the remaining crème fraîche and the milk. If using saffron, grind to a powder and stir in with seasoning to taste. Spoon the mixture evenly over the rolls.

5 Bake in the oven at 200°C (400°F) mark 6 for 25 minutes or until hot and bubbling. Serve immediately.

770 Calories per serving

SUITABLE FOR FREEZING

Chicken Pasta Rolls (above)

TURKEY TETRAZZINI

SERVES 6

225 g (8 oz) dried spaghetti
salt and pepper
75 g (3 oz) butter or margarine
45 ml (3 level tbsp) plain flour
300 ml (½ pint) hot turkey or chicken stock
100 ml (4 fl oz) double cream
45 ml (3 tbsp) dry sherry
1.25 ml (¼ level tsp) freshly grated nutmeg
125 g (4 oz) button mushrooms, wiped and sliced
350–450 g (12 oz–1 lb) cooked turkey, sliced or
cut into bite-sized pieces
30 ml (2 level tbsp) freshly grated
Parmesan cheese

1 Cook the spaghetti in a large saucepan of boiling salted water for 10–12 minutes or until just tender.

2 Meanwhile, make the sauce. Melt half the butter or margarine in a heavy-based saucepan, sprinkle in the flour and stir over gentle heat for 1–2 minutes. Gradually stir in the hot stock, then bring to the boil. Simmer, stirring all the time, until thick and smooth.

3 Remove the sauce from the heat and leave to cool for about 5 minutes, then stir in the cream, sherry and nutmeg. Season with salt and pepper.

4 Melt the remaining butter or margarine in a separate pan. Add the mushrooms and fry gently until soft.

5 Drain the spaghetti and arrange half of it in the base of a greased baking dish.

6 Arrange the turkey and mushrooms over the top. Cover with the remaining spaghetti, then coat with the sauce.

7 Sprinkle with the Parmesan cheese and bake in the oven at 190°C (375°F) mark 5 for 30 minutes or until golden and bubbling.

455 Calories per serving

SUITABLE FOR FREEZING AT THE END OF STEP 6

MACARONI LAYER PIE

SERVES 4-6

15 ml (1 tbsp) vegetable oil
450 g (1 lb) lean minced beef
125 g (4 oz) onion, skinned and chopped
1 garlic clove, skinned and crushed
400 g (14 oz) can of chopped tomatoes
200 ml (7 fl oz) chicken or beef stock
5 ml (1 level tsp) dried mixed herbs
salt and pepper
225 g (8 oz) dried macaroni
40 g (1½ oz) butter
45 ml (3 level tbsp) plain flour
450 ml (¾ pint) milk
10 ml (2 level tsp) Dijon mustard
125 g (4 oz) Cheddar cheese, grated

1 Heat the oil in a medium saucepan, add the mince and onion, and cook over a high heat for 5–8 minutes or until they are lightly coloured. Break up the mince as you brown it, spreading it evenly around the pan, to prevent it forming into lumps.

2 Add the garlic, tomatoes, stock, herbs and seasoning. Bring to the boil, then reduce the heat and simmer, uncovered, for about 20 minutes, or until the mince is tender and the liquid well reduced. Taste and adjust the seasoning.

3 Meanwhile, cook the macaroni in a large saucepan of boiling salted water for 10–12 minutes or until just tender. Drain and rinse under cold running water, then drain for 2–3 minutes longer.

4 Layer the mince and pasta alternately in a lightly greased, large, deep ovenproof serving dish, ending with a pasta layer on the top.

5 Melt the butter in a saucepan, add the flour and cook, stirring, for 1–2 minutes before gradually adding the milk. Bring to the boil, then simmer for 2–3 minutes.

6 Off the heat, whisk in the mustard, half the

grated Cheddar cheese and seasoning. Pour over the pasta.

7 Sprinkle the remaining grated Cheddar over the top of the pie. Stand the dish on a baking tray and bake in the oven at 200°C (400°F) mark 6 for 35–40 minutes or until golden and thoroughly hot. Serve immediately.

830–555 Calories per serving

SUITABLE FOR FREEZING AT THE END OF STEP 6

BEEF AND VEAL CANNELLONI GRATIN

SERVES 4

30 ml (2 tbsp) olive oil

225 g (8 oz) onions, skinned and finely chopped

125 g (4 oz) carrots, peeled and finely chopped

2 celery sticks, trimmed and finely chopped

175 g (6 oz) red pepper, deseeded and finely chopped

225 g (8 oz) each lean minced beef and lean minced veal

40 g (1½ oz) plus 5 ml (1 level tsp) plain flour

300 ml (½ pint) beef stock

150 ml (5 fl oz) red wine

125 g (4 oz) prosciutto (Parma ham), finely chopped

30 ml (2 level tbsp) chopped fresh rosemary

1 bay leaf

salt and pepper

16 dried cannelloni

50 g (2 oz) butter

600 ml (1 pint) milk

50 g (2 oz) Parmesan cheese, freshly grated

1 Heat the oil in a large frying pan, add the onions, carrots, celery and red pepper, and cook until the vegetables soften and begin to colour.

2 Add the beef and veal and cook over a high heat, stirring frequently, until the meat begins to brown. Stir in the 5 ml (1 level tsp) flour and cook for a further minute.

3 Pour in the stock and red wine, and add the prosciutto, rosemary and bay leaf. Season with salt and pepper. Slowly bring to the boil, then cover and simmer gently for about 1 hour or until the mixture has reduced to a thick sauce. (If necessary, uncover the pan, increase the heat and boil to reduce.) Remove the bay leaf.

4 Cook the pasta in a large saucepan of boiling salted water for 10–12 minutes or until tender. Drain well and leave to cool slightly.

5 Fill the cannelloni tubes with the mince mixture and place in a single layer in a 2.4 litre (4 pint) ovenproof serving dish.

6 Melt the butter in a small saucepan. Add the remaining flour and cook, stirring, for 1–2 minutes before gradually adding the milk. Bring to the boil, then reduce the heat and simmer, stirring occasionally, for 2–3 minutes. Off the heat, beat in half the grated cheese and add pepper to taste. Spoon over the pasta.

7 Sprinkle with the remaining cheese and bake in the oven at 180°C (350°F) mark 4 for about 40 minutes or until golden and bubbling. Serve immediately.

VARIATION

If you wish, you can use beef only in this recipe by substituting an extra 225 g (8 oz) beef for the veal.

1000 Calories per serving

SUITABLE FOR FREEZING AT THE END OF STEP 6

SEAFOOD LASAGNE

SERVES 6

450 g (1 lb) fresh haddock fillet, skinned

300 ml (½ pint) white wine

slices of carrot and onion, and a bay leaf
for flavouring

salt and pepper

200 g (7 oz) dried lasagne verde

150 g (5 oz) butter

450 g (1 lb) trimmed leeks, thickly sliced and
washed

1 garlic clove, skinned and crushed

90 g (3½ oz) plain flour

150 ml (5 fl oz) single cream

150 ml (5 fl oz) soured cream

15 ml (1 level tbsp) chopped fresh dill or 2.5 ml
(½ level tsp) dried dill weed

225 g (8 oz) ready-cooked seafood cocktail
(see Cook's Tip on page 98)

50 g (2 oz) Cheddar or Gruyère cheese, grated

30 ml (2 level tbsp) freshly grated
Parmesan cheese

45 ml (3 level tbsp) pine kernels

1 Put the haddock fillet in a frying pan and cover with water and half the wine. Add the flavouring ingredients and season with salt and pepper. Bring to the boil, then reduce the heat, cover and simmer for 5 minutes or until tender.

2 Lift the fish on to a plate and flake the flesh, discarding any bones. Strain the cooking juices and make up to 1 litre (1¾ pints) with water.

3 Cook the lasagne in a large saucepan of boiling salted water for about 12 minutes or until just tender. (Even if you are using no-cook lasagne, you should still boil it for about 7 minutes.) Drain and immediately run cold water over the pasta. Spread on a clean tea towel and cover with a damp tea towel until required.

4 Melt 50 g (2 oz) butter in a medium saucepan, add the leeks and garlic, cover and cook gently for about 10 minutes. Remove from the pan using a slotted spoon.

5 Add the remaining 75 g (3 oz) butter to the pan and melt. Add the flour and cook, stirring, for 1 minute. Off the heat, mix in the reserved 1 litre (1¾ pints) stock and the remaining 150 ml (5 fl oz) wine. Bring to the boil, stirring, and cook for 2 minutes. Off the heat, whisk in the cream, soured cream and dill. Season with salt and pepper.

6 Spoon a little of the sauce into a 3 litre (5¼ pint) shallow ovenproof dish. Top with a layer of pasta, followed by the haddock, seafood cocktail and leeks, and a little more sauce. Continue layering the ingredients, finishing with the sauce. Scatter over the grated Cheddar cheese, Parmesan cheese and pine kernels. Cook in the oven at 200°C (400°F) mark 6 for 45–50 minutes or until piping hot. Cool for 10 minutes before serving.

720 Calories per serving

SUITABLE FOR FREEZING AT THE END OF STEP 6

VARIATIONS

CREAMY CHICKEN LASAGNE

(700 Calories per serving)

Ingredients as for Seafood Lasagne, replacing the haddock and seafood cocktail/prawns with 1.4 kg (2 lb) oven-ready chicken, and the dill with 60 ml (4 level tbsp) chopped fresh basil or 5 ml (1 level tsp) dried basil. Cover the chicken with water, half the wine and the flavourings as in step 1. Bring to the boil, cover and simmer for 1 hour or until tender. Cut the chicken into bite-sized pieces, discarding skin and bone. Bubble down the cooking juices to about 1 litre (1¾ pints). Strain and skim.

Continued on page 98

Seafood Lasagne (above)

Complete the lasagne as in steps 3–7 of Seafood Lasagne, whisking 30 ml (2 level tbsp) Dijon mustard into the sauce in step 5. Alternatively, 450 g (1 lb) ready-cooked chicken or turkey could be used, making the sauce with the wine and 900 ml (1½ pints) good chicken stock.

LEEK AND MUSHROOM LASAGNE

(720 Calories per serving)

Ingredients as for Seafood Lasagne, replacing the haddock and seafood cocktail/prawns with 450 g (1 lb) mixed mushrooms (brown cap, flat, oyster, etc.) and the dill with 60 ml (4 level tbsp) chopped fresh basil or 50 ml (1 level tsp) dried basil. Increase the leeks to 700 g (1½ lb) and Cheddar or Gruyère cheese to 225 g (8 oz). Omit steps 1–2. Continue as in steps 3–4, then sauté the sliced mushrooms in the remaining 75 g (3 oz) butter for 3–4 minutes. Remove from the pan using slotted spoons. Make the sauce as in step 5, adding more butter if necessary and using 750 ml (1¼ pints) vegetable stock and 300 ml (½ pint) white wine with the basil in place of dill. Whisk in 30 ml (2 level tbsp) Dijon mustard. Complete as in steps 6–7, layering the mushrooms and some of the Cheddar or Gruyère cheese in place of the fish.

COOK'S TIP

Look out for packs of chilled or frozen seafood cocktail, available from major supermarkets. They usually include cooked mussels, squid, prawns and sometimes cockles. If you can't find them, simply replace with some cooked, peeled prawns.

*F*ISH-STUFFED CANNELLONI WITH CHEESE

SERVES 4

50 g (2 oz) butter or margarine
125 g (4 oz) mushrooms, wiped and chopped
1 small red pepper, deseeded and diced
1 garlic clove, skinned and crushed
200 g (7 oz) can of salmon or tuna, drained and flaked
50 g (2 oz) fresh breadcrumbs
12 dried cannelloni

FOR THE SAUCE
50 g (2 oz) butter or margarine
60 ml (4 level tbsp) plain flour
600 ml (1 pint) milk
175 g (6 oz) Cheddar cheese, grated
salt and pepper

1 Melt the butter or margarine in a saucepan, add the mushrooms and red pepper, and fry for 2–3 minutes or until soft. Add the garlic, fish and breadcrumbs, and cook for 5 minutes, stirring.

2 To make the sauce, melt the butter or margarine in a saucepan, stir in the flour and cook for 1 minute, stirring. Remove the pan from the heat and gradually stir in the milk. Bring to the boil, then simmer, stirring, until thickened.

3 Remove from the heat and stir in 150 g (5 oz) of the cheese until melted. Season well.

4 Spoon the fish filling into the cannelloni so that it protrudes slightly at each end.

5 Pour enough sauce into an ovenproof serving dish to just cover the bottom. Arrange the cannelloni side by side in the dish and pour the remaining sauce over them.

6 Sprinkle the rest of the cheese over the top. Bake in the oven at 200°C (400°F) mark 6 for 20 minutes or until golden. Serve immediately.

860 Calories per serving

SUITABLE FOR FREEZING AT THE END OF STEP 5

SMOKED-FISH GRATIN

SERVE 8

900 g (2 lb) smoked haddock fillet
750 ml (1¼ pints) milk
butter
900 g (2 lb) trimmed leeks, sliced and washed
salt and pepper
150 ml (5 fl oz) double cream
225 g (8 oz) cooked peeled prawns
125 g (4 oz) small dried pasta shapes, such as
penne ('quills') or farfalle (bows)
10 ml (2 tsp) oil
50 g (2 oz) plain flour
125 g (4 oz) Cheddar cheese, grated
15 ml (1 level tbsp) Dijon mustard
30 ml (2 level tbsp) chopped fresh parsley
2 egg whites
flat-leafed parsley sprigs and king prawns,
to garnish

1 Place the fish in a roasting tin or large frying pan. Pour over about 600 ml (1 pint) milk. Slowly bring to the boil, cover and simmer gently for 10–15 minutes or until tender. Remove the fish from the milk and cool slightly. Strain the milk into a jug and reserve. Flake the fish into a bowl, discarding skin and bones.

2 Melt 50 g (2 oz) butter in a pan, add the leeks and cook for 10 minutes or until very soft but not brown. Season with salt and pepper, and stir in the cream. Add to the haddock with the prawns.

3 Cook the pasta in a large saucepan of boiling salted water for about 8 minutes or until just tender. Drain, then stir in the oil.

4 Rinse out the pasta pan, then melt 50 g (2 oz) butter in it. Off the heat, stir in the flour and gradually add the reserved milk and remaining milk. Bring to the boil, stirring. Boil for 2 minutes, then remove from the heat and stir in 50 g (2 oz) cheese, the mustard and parsley.

5 Mix the pasta with the leek and fish mixture and place in one 3.4 litre (6 pint) or two 2 litre (3½ pint) ovenproof dishes. Whisk the egg whites until they stand in stiff peaks. Gently fold into the cheese sauce, then pour over the leek and pasta mixture. Sprinkle with the remaining cheese. Cook in the oven at 200°C (400°F) mark 6 for 40–45 minutes or until golden brown. Garnish with flat-leafed parsley and prawns.

530 Calories per serving

NOT SUITABLE FOR FREEZING

COOK'S TIP

Although this gratin is not suitable for freezing, it can be prepared ahead up to the end of step 4, then cooled and refrigerated (pasta and fish mixture separately) overnight. When completing, warm the cheese sauce gently before adding the whisked egg whites.

SPINACH AND RICOTTA CANNELLONI

SERVES 4–6

60 ml (4 tbsp) olive oil

2 small onions, skinned and finely chopped

30 ml (2 level tbsp) tomato purée

5 ml (1 level tsp) mild paprika

two 400 g (14 oz) cans of chopped tomatoes

pinch of dried oregano

300 ml (½ pint) dry red wine or vegetable stock

large pinch of sugar

salt and pepper

1 garlic clove, skinned and crushed

450 g (1 lb) frozen leaf spinach, thawed and drained

450 g (1 lb) ricotta cheese

freshly grated nutmeg

18 small sheets of fresh lasagne

freshly grated Parmesan cheese or a few breadcrumbs

1 To make the sauce, heat half the oil in a heavy-based saucepan, add half the onion and fry for 5–10 minutes or until very soft. Add the tomato purée and paprika and fry for 2–3 minutes. Add the tomatoes, oregano, red wine or stock and sugar, and season with salt and pepper. Simmer for 20 minutes.

2 Heat the remaining oil in a large saucepan, add the garlic and remaining onion and cook for 5 minutes, stirring all the time. Add the spinach and cook for 2 minutes. Cool slightly, then add the ricotta cheese. Season with nutmeg, salt and pepper.

3 Lay the lasagne sheets on a work surface and divide the spinach mixture between them. Roll up the sheets to enclose the filling and arrange, seam-side down in a single layer, in a greased ovenproof dish. Pour the sauce over and sprinkle with Parmesan cheese or breadcrumbs. Bake in the oven at 200°C (400°F) mark 6 for 30 minutes.

COOK'S TIP

If you can't buy sheets of fresh lasagne, use dried, but cook them first according to packet instructions and reduce the final cooking time to about 20 minutes.

535–355 Calories per serving

SUITABLE FOR FREEZING

Spinach and Ricotta Cannelloni (above)

Stuffed Baked Pasta Shells

Serves 4–6

90 g (3½ oz) butter or margarine

175 g (6 oz) salted cashew nuts,
roughly chopped

175 g (6 oz) button mushrooms, wiped and
roughly chopped

1 small onion, skinned and roughly chopped

50 g (2 oz) celery, trimmed and roughly chopped

225 g (8 oz) fresh spinach

salt and pepper

24 large dried pasta shells

35 g (1¼ oz) plain flour

750 ml (1¼ pints) milk

1 bay leaf

275 g (10 oz) Lancashire cheese, coarsely grated

45 ml (3 level tbsp) chopped fresh parsley

1 egg

1 Melt 50 g (2 oz) butter or margarine in a large frying pan. Add the cashew nuts, mushrooms, onion and celery, and fry for about 10 minutes or until golden and any excess liquid has evaporated, stirring occasionally.

2 Wash the spinach, put in a saucepan, cover and cook over a low heat until just wilted. Drain well, then roughly chop. Stir into the mixture, season and leave to cool.

3 Cook the pasta shells in a large saucepan of boiling salted water for about 10 minutes or until just tender. Drain well. Fill the shells with the nut mixture and place in a single layer in a large, shallow ovenproof dish.

4 Melt the remaining butter or margarine in a small saucepan. Add the flour and cook, stirring, for 1–2 minutes, then remove from the heat and gradually blend in the milk. Add the bay leaf, then bring to the boil and simmer, stirring, for 2–3 minutes. Remove from the heat and discard the bay leaf, then beat in the cheese, parsley and egg.

Season with salt and pepper and spoon evenly over the pasta.

5 Bake at 180°C (350°F) mark 4 for about 40 minutes or until golden and bubbling.

COOK'S TIP

You will need very large pasta shells for this recipe, measuring about 4 cm (1½ inches) long before cooking; once cooked they are even bigger. Don't be tempted to use small shells – you will run out of patience trying to stuff them.

1290–860 Calories per serving

SUITABLE FOR FREEZING AT THE END OF STEP 4

Pasta Pie

Serves 6

125 g (4 oz) butter

30 ml (2 tbsp) olive oil

1 small onion, skinned and finely chopped

2 garlic cloves, skinned and crushed

400 g (14 oz) can of tomatoes

5 ml (1 level tsp) chopped fresh basil

salt and pepper

225 g (8 oz) dried pasta, such as macaroni

75 g (3 oz) plain flour

600 ml (1 pint) milk

75 g (3 oz) Gruyère cheese, grated

60 ml (4 level tbsp) freshly grated
Parmesan cheese

45 ml (3 level tbsp) dried breadcrumbs

1 Melt 50 g (2 oz) of the butter in a heavy-based saucepan with the oil. Add the onion and garlic, and fry gently for 5 minutes or until soft.

2 Add the tomatoes, basil and seasoning to taste, then stir with a wooden spoon to break up the tomatoes. Bring to the boil, then lower the heat and simmer for 10 minutes, stirring occasionally.

3 Meanwhile, cook the pasta in a large saucepan of boiling salted water for 10–12 minutes or until just tender. Drain well.

4 Melt the remaining butter in a separate saucepan, add the flour and cook over a low heat, stirring, for about 2 minutes. Remove from the heat and gradually blend in the milk. Bring to the boil slowly, stirring, until the sauce thickens. Add the Gruyère cheese and seasoning to taste and stir until melted.

5 Mix the pasta with the tomato sauce. Arrange half in a large, buttered ovenproof serving dish.

6 Pour over half of the cheese sauce. Repeat the layers, then sprinkle evenly with the Parmesan cheese and breadcrumbs.

7 Bake in the oven at 190°C (375°F) mark 5 for 15 minutes, then brown under a hot grill for 5 minutes. Serve immediately.

575 Calories per serving

SUITABLE FOR FREEZING

CREAMY PASTA BAKE

SERVES 4

175 g (6 oz) dried pasta shapes,
such as penne ('quills')
salt and pepper
olive oil
125 g (4 oz) onion, skinned and finely chopped
1 garlic clove, skinned and crushed
300 ml (10 fl oz) single cream
2 eggs
175 g (6 oz) Gruyère cheese, coarsely grated

1 Cook the pasta in a large saucepan of boiling salted water for 10–12 minutes or until just tender. Drain well and toss in a little oil.

2 Heat 15 ml (1 tbsp) oil in a small frying pan, add the onion and garlic, and fry for a few minutes or until the mixture is beginning to soften.

3 In a large bowl, whisk together the cream and the eggs, then season generously. Stir in the cheese, the onion mixture and the cooked pasta.

4 Spoon into a 1.1 litre (2 pint) ovenproof dish. Stand the dish on a baking tray and bake in the oven at 190°C (375°F) mark 5 for 35–40 minutes or until the top is golden brown.

550 Calories per serving

NOT SUITABLE FOR FREEZING

VEGETABLE LASAGNE

SERVES 6

30 ml (2 tbsp) olive oil

1 garlic clove, skinned and crushed

1 carrot, peeled and chopped

1 large onion, skinned and sliced

1 red pepper, deseeded and chopped

15 ml (1 level tbsp) mild paprika

10 ml (2 level tsp) dried oregano or marjoram

1 large aubergine, trimmed and cut into large chunks

225 g (8 oz) button mushrooms, wiped and sliced

2 large courgettes, trimmed and sliced

two 400 g (14 oz) cans of chopped tomatoes

30 ml (2 level tbsp) tomato purée

2 bay leaves

about 350 g (12 oz) fresh lasagne or 225 g (8 oz) dried lasagne

salt and pepper

900 ml (1½ pints) Béchamel Sauce (see page 86)

Parmesan or Cheddar cheese, freshly grated (optional)

1 Heat the oil in a large saucepan. Add the garlic, carrot, onion and red pepper, and fry for 1–2 minutes. Add the paprika, herbs and aubergine and fry for a few minutes more.

2 Add the remaining vegetables to the pan with the tomatoes, tomato purée and bay leaves. Bring to the boil, cover and simmer for 30 minutes.

3 Meanwhile, if using dried lasagne that needs pre-cooking, cook it in boiling salted water according to packet instructions. Drain and leave to dry on a clean tea-towel.

4 Spread a small amount of the tomato sauce in the base of a 2.8 litre (5 pint) ovenproof dish. Cover with a layer of lasagne and top with a layer of béchamel sauce. Continue layering in this way, ending with a layer of béchamel sauce that covers the pasta completely. Sprinkle with the cheese.

5 Bake the lasagne in the oven at 200°C (400°F) mark 6 for 45 minutes–1 hour or until the lasagne is piping hot and well browned. Leave to stand for 15 minutes before serving.

285 Calories per serving

SUITABLE FOR FREEZING

TORTELLINI AL FORNO

SERVES 4

450 g (1 lb) aubergines, trimmed and chopped

salt and pepper

25 g (1 oz) butter or margarine

450 g (1 lb) tomatoes, skinned and chopped

1 garlic clove, skinned and crushed

225 g (8 oz) fresh or dried tortellini

150 ml (5 fl oz) milk

225 g (8 oz) full-fat soft cheese

15 ml (1 level tbsp) grated Parmesan cheese

30 ml (2 level tbsp) dried breadcrumbs

1 Sprinkle the aubergines with salt and leave for 15–20 minutes. Rinse well and pat dry.

2 Melt the butter or margarine in a frying pan, add the aubergines, tomatoes and garlic and cook gently for 5–10 minutes or until very soft. Season.

3 Cook the tortellini in boiling salted water for 10–12 minutes (for dried pasta) or 3–4 minutes (for fresh pasta) or until just tender. Drain well.

4 Spoon the vegetable mixture into a shallow ovenproof dish. Layer the tortellini on top.

5 In a bowl, gradually beat the milk into the cheese, whisking until smooth. Stir in 5 ml (1 level tsp) Parmesan. Spoon over the tortellini. Sprinkle the top with breadcrumbs and remaining cheese.

6 Bake in the oven at 200°C (400°F) mark 6 for 25–30 minutes or until the top is golden.

520 Calories per serving

SUITABLE FOR FREEZING

Vegetable Lasagne (above)

Mushroom Lasagne

SERVES 6

225 g (8 oz) frozen leaf spinach, thawed
salt and pepper
olive oil
about 350 g (12 oz) fresh lasagne or 225 g (8 oz) dried lasagne
900 g (2 lb) mixed mushrooms, such as button, flat and brown-top (chestnut), wiped
125 g (4 oz) butter or margarine
30 ml (2 tbsp) lemon juice
75 g (3 oz) plain flour
600 ml (1 pint) milk
600 ml (1 pint) vegetable stock
freshly grated nutmeg, to taste
2 large garlic cloves, skinned and crushed
175 g (6 oz) Gruyère cheese, grated
50 g (2 oz) fresh white breadcrumbs

1 Drain the spinach and squeeze out any excess liquid. Chop finely.

2 Bring a large saucepan of salted water to the boil. (Use two if necessary.) Add a dash of olive oil to each, followed by the lasagne. Cook according to packet instructions, stirring occasionally. When the pasta is tender, drain it in a colander and immediately run cold water over it. This will stop the pasta from cooking further and will rinse off some of the starch. Spread the pasta out on clean tea-towels and cover with a damp tea-towel until required.

3 Quarter or slice the mushrooms, or leave them whole, depending on their size. Melt half the butter or margarine in a large saucepan. Add the mushrooms and lemon juice, and season with salt and pepper. Cover and cook over a fairly high heat for 4–6 minutes or until the mushrooms are tender. Remove from the pan with a slotted spoon, then bubble the juices to evaporate any excess moisture until there is only fat left in the saucepan.

4 Melt the remaining butter or margarine in the same saucepan. Carefully stir in the flour and cook for 1–2 minutes before slowly blending in the milk and stock. Gradually bring to the boil, making sure that you keep stirring all the time, and cook for 1–2 minutes or until boiling and thickened. Mix in the nutmeg, garlic and spinach. Taste and adjust the seasoning if necessary.

5 Spoon a little of the sauce into the base of a 2.8 litre (5 pint) ovenproof dish. Top with a layer of pasta followed by a layer of mushrooms. Spoon over more of the sauce, then continue layering the ingredients, finishing with the sauce, making sure that it completely covers the ingredients underneath. Sprinkle over the Gruyère cheese and breadcrumbs.

6 Stand the dish on a baking tray and cook in the oven at 200°C (400°F) mark 6 for 45 minutes–1 hour.

590 Calories per serving

SUITABLE FOR FREEZING

Macaroni and Broccoli Cheese

SERVES 2

75 g (3 oz) wholewheat macaroni
salt and pepper
25 g (1 oz) butter
25 g (1 oz) plain flour
300 ml (½ pint) milk
75 g (3 oz) Red Leicester cheese, grated
125 g (4 oz) broccoli florets
15 ml (1 tbsp) fresh wholemeal breadcrumbs

1 Cook the macaroni in a large saucepan of boiling salted water for 15 minutes or until tender.

2 Meanwhile, put the butter, flour and milk in a saucepan. Heat, whisking continuously, until the sauce boils, thickens and is smooth. Simmer for 1–2 minutes.

3 Remove the pan from the heat, add most of the cheese and stir until melted. Season with salt and pepper.

4 Blanch the broccoli in boiling water for 7 minutes or until tender. Drain well.

5 Put the broccoli in the base of a 900 ml (1½ pint) flameproof serving dish. Drain the macaroni and arrange over the broccoli with the cheese sauce. Sprinkle with the remaining cheese and the breadcrumbs. Brown under a hot grill.

COOK'S TIP

The flavour of wholewheat pasta is stronger and nuttier than the 'white' variety.

560 Calories per serving

SUITABLE FOR FREEZING

☙❧

Macaroni Bake

SERVES 4–6

175 g (6 oz) dried macaroni
salt and pepper
30 ml (2 tbsp) olive oil
125 g (4 oz) onion, skinned and chopped
225 g (8 oz) button mushrooms, wiped and sliced
350 g (12 oz) tomatoes, skinned and chopped
300 ml (½ pint) vegetable stock
15 ml (1 level tbsp) tomato purée
5 ml (1 level tsp) dried mixed herbs
5 ml (1 level tsp) dried oregano
30 ml (2 level tbsp) plain wholemeal flour
300 ml (½ pint) milk

125 g (4 oz) low-fat soft cheese
1 egg, beaten
5 ml (1 level tsp) English mustard powder
30 ml (2 level tbsp) wholemeal breadcrumbs
30 ml (2 level tbsp) grated Parmesan cheese

1 Cook the pasta in a large saucepan of boiling salted water for 10–12 minutes or until just tender. Drain well.

2 Heat the oil in a separate pan, add the onion and fry gently for 5 minutes or until soft.

3 Add the mushrooms to the pan, increase the heat and toss with the onion for 1–2 minutes.

4 Add the tomatoes and stock and bring to the boil, stirring constantly to break up the tomatoes. Lower the heat and stir in the tomato purée, herbs and salt and pepper to taste. Simmer gently for 10 minutes.

5 Put the flour and milk in a food processor and blend for 1 minute. Transfer to a heavy-based saucepan and simmer until thickened.

6 Remove from the heat and beat in the cheese, egg, mustard and salt and pepper to taste.

7 Mix the macaroni with the mushrooms in the tomato sauce, then pour into an ovenproof serving dish. Pour over the cheese sauce. Sprinkle with breadcrumbs and Parmesan cheese.

8 Bake in the oven at 190°C (375°F) mark 5 for 20 minutes or until golden and bubbling. Serve immediately.

450–300 Calories per serving

SUITABLE FOR FREEZING

☙❧

Roasted Vegetable and Pasta Gratin

Serves 8

450 g (1 lb) aubergines, trimmed and cut into
bite-sized pieces

700 g (1½ lb) mixed peppers, deseeded and cut
into bite-sized pieces

450 g (1 lb) squash, such as butternut or
pumpkin, peeled and cut into bite-sized pieces

90 ml (6 tbsp) olive oil

225 g (8 oz) dried pasta shapes

450 g (1 lb) frozen leaf spinach, thawed

50 g (2 oz) butter

50 g (2 oz) plain flour

900 ml (1½ pints) milk

30 ml (2 level tbsp) wholegrain mustard

150 g (5 oz) full-fat soft cheese with garlic
and herbs

225 g (8 oz) mature Cheddar cheese, grated

salt and pepper

1 Put the aubergine, peppers and squash in two roasting tins with the oil. Roast in the oven at 220°C (425°F) mark 7 for 45 minutes or until tender and charred.

2 Meanwhile, cook the pasta shapes in a large saucepan of boiling salted water for 10–12 minutes or until just tender. Drain thoroughly. Squeeze the excess liquid from the frozen spinach.

3 Melt the butter in a saucepan and stir in the flour. Cook, stirring, for 1 minute before adding the milk. Bring to the boil, stirring all the time. Simmer for 2-3 minutes or until the sauce thickens. Off the heat, add the mustard, soft cheese and 175 g (6 oz) of the Cheddar. Stir thoroughly until smooth. Season well with salt and pepper.

4 Mix the pasta, spinach and roasted vegetables with the sauce and spoon into a large, shallow ovenproof dish. Sprinkle the remaining Cheddar cheese over the top.

5 Stand the dish on a baking tray and cook in the oven at 200°C (400°F) mark 6 for about 40 min-

utes or until hot and golden brown, covering with foil, if necessary, to prevent overbrowning.

VARIATIONS

This dish is a very great way of using up leftovers. You can add cooked ham, chicken or spicy sausage. Any variety of cheese can be used; for a special vegetarian meal, add goats' cheese or Stilton.

585 Calories per serving

SUITABLE FOR FREEZING AT THE END OF STEP 4

Roasted Vegetable and Pasta Gratin (above)

CAULIFLOWER, LEEK AND MACARONI CHEESE

SERVES 4

1 cauliflower, about 900 g (2 lb), divided into florets

salt and pepper

75 g (3 oz) dried macaroni

225 g (8 oz) leeks, trimmed, thickly sliced and washed

50 g (2 oz) butter or margarine

15 ml (1 level tbsp) chopped fresh thyme

50 g (2 oz) plain flour

750 ml (1¼ pints) milk

150 g (5 oz) Cheddar cheese, grated

30 ml (2 level tbsp) freshly grated Parmesan cheese

60 ml (4 level tbsp) fresh brown breadcrumbs

60 ml (4 level tbsp) coarse or medium oatmeal

1 Put the cauliflower florets in a large saucepan of boiling salted water with the macaroni. Boil for 5 minutes. Add the leeks and boil for about another 5 minutes or until all are just tender. Drain well.

2 Melt the butter or margarine in a medium saucepan. Stir in the thyme, flour and milk. Bring to the boil and cook, whisking continuously, until slightly thickened. Off the heat, stir in half of the grated Cheddar cheese and half of the Parmesan cheese. Season with salt and pepper.

3 Stir the vegetable and macaroni mixture into the sauce. Spoon into a large, shallow ovenproof dish and sprinkle over the breadcrumbs, oatmeal and remaining grated cheese.

4 Bake in the oven at 180°C (350°F) mark 4 for about 35 minutes or until piping hot. Brown under a hot grill if necessary.

VARIATION

Substitute 20 ml (4 level tsp) English mustard powder for the chopped thyme to give the sauce a slightly tangy flavour that complements the cauliflower, cheese and leek flavours well.

700 Calories per serving

SUITABLE FOR FREEZING

PASTA AND MUSHROOMS BAKED WITH TWO CHEESES

SERVES 2–3

225 g (8 oz) dried tagliatelle or other noodles

salt and pepper

25 g (1 oz) butter

1 garlic clove, skinned and crushed

225 g (8 oz) mushrooms, wiped and thinly sliced

50 g (2 oz) Stilton cheese

60 ml (4 tbsp) double cream

1 egg, lightly beaten

125 g (4 oz) Mozzarella cheese, grated

1 Cook the pasta in a large saucepan of boiling salted water for 10–12 minutes or until just tender. Drain well.

2 Meanwhile, melt the butter in a large frying pan, add the garlic and mushrooms and cook for about 5 minutes or until just softened, stirring frequently.

3 Crumble in the Stilton cheese and cook for 2–3 minutes, stirring continuously. Stir in the cream and season with salt and pepper.

4 Season the pasta with lots of pepper and mix into the mushroom sauce. Stir in the egg and mix together thoroughly.

5 Spoon the mixture into a buttered ovenproof serving dish and sprinkle the Mozzarella on top. Cover with foil and bake in the oven at 180°C (350°F) mark 4 for 10 minutes, then remove the oil and bake at 220°C (425°F) mark 7 for a further

10–15 minutes or until brown and crusty on top. Serve immediately.

955–635 Calories per serving

NOT SUITABLE FOR FREEZING

Pasta and Aubergine Gratin

SERVES 4

30 ml (2 tbsp) olive oil
1 onion, skinned and chopped
1 garlic clove, skinned and crushed
10 ml (2 tsp) mild paprika
10 ml (2 tsp) tomato purée
350 g (12 oz) aubergine, trimmed and roughly chopped
400 g (14 oz) can of chopped tomatoes
5 ml (1 level tsp) sugar
2 small courgettes, trimmed and thinly sliced
salt and pepper
275 g (10 oz) dried rigatoni or other pasta shapes
15 ml (1 level tbsp) pesto sauce
150 g (5 oz) Gruyère or mature Cheddar cheese
25 g (1 oz) freshly grated Parmesan cheese

1 Heat the oil in a heavy-based saucepan, add the onion and garlic, and fry for about 5 minutes or until softened. Add the paprika and tomato purée and cook, stirring, for 1 minute. Add the aubergine and cook for a further 2 minutes, stirring to coat in the tomato and onion mixture.
2 Add the tomatoes, sugar and 75 ml (5 tbsp) water. Bring to the boil, then cover, reduce the heat and simmer for about 15 minutes or until the aubergine is just tender. Add the courgettes, re-cover and cook for a further 5 minutes. Season the aubergine and courgette mixture with plenty of salt and pepper.
3 Meanwhile, cook the pasta in a large saucepan of boiling salted water for 10–12 minutes or until just tender. Drain the pasta and return it to the pan. Add the pesto sauce and toss to coat.
4 Toss the pasta with the aubergine sauce and check the seasoning. Transfer to a gratin dish and top with the cheeses. Bake in the oven at 200°C (400°F) mark 6 for about 20 minutes or until golden brown and bubbling.

565 Calories per serving

NOT SUITABLE FOR FREEZING

RATATOUILLE PASTA BAKE

SERVES 4–6

30 ml (2 tbsp) olive oil

1 large onion, skinned and thinly sliced

1 red pepper, deseeded and cut into 5 cm
(2 inch) strips

1 yellow pepper, deseeded and cut into 5 cm
(2 inch) strips

225 g (8 oz) courgettes, trimmed and cut into
5 cm (2 inch) strips

450 g (1 lb) ripe tomatoes, skinned and chopped

2 garlic cloves, skinned and crushed

30 ml (2 level tbsp) tomato purée

30 ml (2 level tbsp) chopped fresh basil or 5 ml
(1 level tsp) dried basil

pinch of sugar

salt and pepper

450 ml (¾ pint) vegetable stock

350 g (12 oz) mixed coloured pasta twists

50 g (2 oz) butter

175 g (6 oz) mature Cheddar cheese, grated

1 Heat the oil in a large saucepan, add the onion and peppers, and cook for 5 minutes or until softened, stirring. Add the courgettes and cook for 5 minutes.

2 Stir in the tomatoes, garlic, tomato purée, basil and sugar. Season with salt and pepper and simmer for 25–30 minutes, stirring occasionally and gradually adding the stock.

3 Meanwhile, cook the pasta in a large saucepan of boiling salted water for 10–12 minutes or until just tender. Drain, then return to the pan, add the butter, toss well and season with salt and pepper. Transfer to a deep flameproof dish.

4 Pour the ratatouille sauce over the pasta and sprinkle over the cheese. Grill until golden.

715-475 Calories per serving

NOT SUITABLE FOR FREEZING

*S*ALADS

*I*NSALATA DI MARE

SERVES 6

225 g (8 oz) dried pasta twists
salt and pepper
1 small red pepper, quartered and deseeded
two 227 g (8 oz) packs ready-prepared seafood
cocktail (see page 98)
6 black and 6 green olives, pitted and quartered

FOR THE DRESSING

60 ml (4 tbsp) balsamic or white wine vinegar
150 ml (5 fl oz) olive oil
2 garlic cloves, skinned and crushed
45 ml (3 level tbsp) chopped fresh parsley
salt and pepper
flat-leafed parsley sprigs, to garnish

1 Cook the pasta in a large saucepan of boiling salted water for 10–12 minutes or until just tender. Drain, rinse under cold running water and drain again, then leave to cool.

2 Meanwhile, grill the pepper, skin-side up, for 5–8 minutes until the skin is blistering and beginning to blacken. Place the pepper quarters in a polythene bag, seal tightly and leave to cool.

3 Place the seafood cocktail in a large bowl, add the olives and set aside.

4 To make the dressing, whisk together the vinegar, olive oil, garlic and parsley and season with salt and pepper. Pour over the seafood mixture and leave to marinate at room temperature for 20 minutes.

5 When the pepper is cool, peel off the skin, rinse the pepper under cold water and pat dry with absorbent kitchen paper. Shred finely and add to the seafood with the pasta. Toss lightly to mix. Garnish with flat-leafed parsley sprigs and serve.

445 Calories per serving

NOT SUITABLE FOR FREEZING

Mixed Pasta Salad

SERVES 4

450 g (1 lb) firm white fish fillet, skinned and cut
into chunks

450 g (1 lb) fennel, halved and sliced

150 ml (5 fl oz) dry vermouth

75 ml (5 tbsp) water

salt and pepper

175 g (6 oz) dried pasta shapes, red and green
mixed, such as shells, bows and spirals

450 g (1 lb) tomatoes, skinned, deseeded and
chopped, with the juices reserved

45 ml (3 tbsp) olive oil

45 ml (3 level tbsp) chopped fresh dill or fennel

1 Place the fish, fennel, vermouth and water in a frying pan. Season with salt and pepper, and bring slowly to the boil. Reduce the heat, cover and simmer for 5 minutes or until the fish is tender and flakes easily.

2 Meanwhile, cook the pasta in a large saucepan of boiling salted water for 10–12 minutes or until just tender. Drain well.

3 Using a slotted spoon, lift the fish and fennel out of the cooking liquid. Place in a large bowl with the pasta and tomatoes.

4 Add the tomato juices to the fish liquid, then boil until 175 ml (6 fl oz) remains.

5 Stir in the oil and season with salt and pepper. Mix half into the pasta with the herbs. Cover and leave in a cool place for 1–2 hours.

6 Before serving, stir in the remaining dressing.

455 Calories per serving

NOT SUITABLE FOR FREEZING

Warm Pasta Salad

SERVES 4

350 g (12 oz) dried pasta twists

salt and pepper

1 red pepper, deseeded and chopped

1 green pepper, deseeded and chopped

200 g (7 oz) can of tuna steaks in brine,
drained and flaked

45 ml (3 tbsp) natural yogurt

green salad with a squeeze of lemon juice, to
serve

1 Cook the pasta in a large saucepan of boiling salted water for 10–12 minutes or until just tender. Drain well.

2 Place the warm pasta in a serving dish and stir in the chopped peppers, tuna and yogurt. Season with plenty of pepper.

3 Serve immediately with a green salad, sharpened with a squeeze of lemon juice.

415 Calories per serving

NOT SUITABLE FOR FREEZING

PARTY PASTA

SERVES 6

225 g (8 oz) dried pasta shapes, such as quills, shells or spirals

salt and pepper

225 g (8 oz) thin asparagus spears, trimmed and cut into finger-length pieces

225 g (8 oz) courgettes, coarsely grated

125 g (4 oz) Gruyère cheese, grated

125 g (4 oz) feta cheese, diced

FOR THE DRESSING

150 ml (5 fl oz) olive oils

30 ml (2 tbsp) white wine vinegar

2.5 ml (½ level tsp) sugar

10 ml (2 level tsp) Dijon mustard

30 ml (2 level tbsp) chopped fresh herbs

1 Cook the pasta in boiling salted water for 10–12 minutes, or until just tender. Drain and rinse under cold running water.

2 Cook the asparagus in boiling salted water for 5–7 minutes, or until just tender. Drain and rinse as above.

3 Whisk together all the dressing ingredients and season.

4 Toss together all the ingredients. Serve immediately, or refrigerate, covered, for up to 1 day. Stir before serving.

500 Calories per serving

NOT SUITABLE FOR FREEZING

PASTA SALAD WITH AVOCADO

SERVES 4

125 g (4 oz) dried wholewheat shapes, such as bows or shells

salt and pepper

45 ml (3 tbsp) olive oil

15 ml (1 tbsp) lemon juice

45 ml (3 level tbsp) chopped fresh parsley

15 ml (1 level tbsp) Dijon mustard

225 g (8 oz) smoked back bacon rashers, derinded

225 g (8 oz) cherry tomatoes, halved

2 ripe avocados

1 bunch of watercress, to serve

1 Cook the pasta in a large saucepan of boiling salted water for 10–12 minutes or until just tender. Drain well.

2 Meanwhile, whisk together the oil, lemon juice, parsley, seasoning and mustard.

3 Pour the dressing over the cooked warm pasta and set aside to cool. Grill the bacon until crispy. Snip into pieces and add to the pasta with the tomatoes.

4 Just before serving, peel and dice the avocado flesh and stir gently into the salad. Serve on a bed of watercress.

COOK'S TIP

Stir the avocado into the pasta at the last minute to prevent it breaking up.

475 Calories per serving

NOT SUITABLE FOR FREEZING

Pasta Salad with Avocado Dressing

SERVES 6

225 g (8 oz) dried pasta shapes
salt and pepper
125 g (4 oz) asparagus, trimmed, tips removed
and stalks cut into 2.5 cm (1 inch) pieces
2 courgettes, trimmed and sliced
1 large ripe avocado
200 g (7 oz) very low-fat fromage frais
15 ml (1 tbsp) lemon juice
1 garlic clove, skinned and crushed
1 eating apple
30 ml (2 level tbsp) chopped fresh coriander
15 g (½ oz) shelled pistachios, chopped

1 Cook the pasta in a large saucepan of boiling salted water for 10–12 minutes or until just tender. About 7 minutes before the end of the cooking time, add the asparagus stalk pieces. Add the courgettes and asparagus tips 2–3 minutes before the end of the cooking time.

2 When the pasta is cooked, drain well, rinse under cold running water, then drain well again. Place in a large bowl.

3 Cut the avocado in half, remove the stone, then scoop out the flesh from one half and mash in a bowl. Add the fromage frais, lemon juice, garlic and salt and pepper and mix well together.

4 Chop the remaining avocado half into small pieces. Core and chop the apple. Pour the avocado dressing over the pasta and add the chopped avocado and apple. Toss together until mixed, then sprinkle with the coriander and pistachios. Serve at once.

240 Calories per serving

NOT SUITABLE FOR FREEZING

Pasta and Prawn Salad

SERVES 6

175 g (6 oz) dried pasta shells
salt and pepper
150 ml (5 fl oz) unsweetened apple juice
5 ml (1 level tsp) chopped fresh mint
5 ml (1 tsp) white wine vinegar
225 g (8 oz) crisp eating apples
225 g (8 oz) cooked peeled prawns
shredded lettuce leaves
paprika, to garnish

1 Cook the pasta in a large saucepan of boiling salted water for 10–12 minutes or until just tender. Drain well.

2 Whisk together the apple juice, mint, vinegar and salt and pepper to taste.

3 Core and slice the apples. Stir the prawns, apples and pasta into the dressing until well mixed. Cover and refrigerate for 2–3 hours.

4 Before serving, add the shredded lettuce and toss well. Divide between six plates and dust with paprika to serve.

170 Calories per serving

NOT SUITABLE FOR FREEZING

Pasta and Prawn Salad (above)

Pasta and Anchovy Salad with Garlic Dressing

SERVES 4

two 50 g (2 oz) cans of anchovies in oil, drained
45 ml (3 tbsp) milk
350 g (12 oz) small dried pasta shapes
salt and pepper
1 garlic clove, skinned and roughly chopped
45 ml (3 tbsp) olive oil
juice of ½ lemon
1 red pepper, deseeded and cut into thin strips
60 ml (4 tbsp) mayonnaise

1 Place the anchovies in a bowl and cover with the milk. Soak for 30 minutes to remove salt.

2 Meanwhile, cook the pasta in a large saucepan of boiling salted water for 10–12 minutes or until just tender. Drain well.

3 Drain the anchovies and rinse under cold running water. Pat dry with absorbent kitchen paper.

4 Reserve a few of the anchovies whole for garnishing and pound the remainder to a paste in a pestle and mortar with the garlic. Add the oil and lemon juice gradually, whisking with a fork until thick. Add pepper to taste.

5 Place the pasta in a large bowl. Pour in the dressing immediately and toss well to mix. Leave to cool, then cover and chill for at least 2 hours, or overnight if more convenient.

6 Add the red pepper strips to the pasta salad, reserving a few for garnish. Add the mayonnaise and toss gently to mix. Adjust the seasoning.

7 Pile the salad into a serving bowl and arrange the remaining whole anchovies and red pepper strips in a lattice pattern over the top. Serve at room temperature.

595 Calories per serving

NOT SUITABLE FOR FREEZING

Smoked Mackerel and Pasta Salad

SERVES 4

225 g (8 oz) dried pasta shapes, such as shells or spirals
salt and pepper
3 medium courgettes, about 275 g (10 oz) total weight, sliced
2 oranges
45 ml (3 tbsp) olive oil
350 g (12 oz) smoked mackerel fillets, flaked
snipped chives, to garnish

1 Cook the pasta in boiling salted water for 10–12 minutes, or until just tender. Drain well. Cook the courgettes in boiling salted water for 2–3 minutes or until just tender.

2 Meanwhile, grate the rind of the oranges and reserve. Using a serrated knife, peel and segment the oranges, holding over a bowl to catch the juice.

3 Whisk together the oil, orange rind and juice. Season well and stir in the cooked pasta; cool.

4 Combine all the ingredients with the flaked mackerel, adjust the seasoning and garnish with snipped chives.

525 Calories per serving

NOT SUITABLE FOR FREEZING

VARIATION

You could also use canned salmon, tuna or sardines, or smoked trout – just keep the quantities the same.

Pasta with Feta and Cauliflower Salad

Serves 4

½ medium cauliflower, broken into florets
a handful of fresh mint
125 g (4 oz) wholewheat pasta twists or shells
salt and pepper
50 g (2 oz) feta cheese

FOR THE DRESSING

30 ml (2 tbsp) lemon juice
10 ml (2 tsp) olive oil
pepper

1 Steam the cauliflower with a couple of sprigs of mint for about 8 minutes or until tender. Drain well and put into a bowl.

2 Cook the pasta in a large saucepan of boiling salted water for 10–12 minutes or until just tender. Drain and add to the cauliflower. Crumble the feta over the cauliflower and pasta. Chop a few sprigs of fresh mint and add to the salad.

3 For the dressing, mix together the lemon juice, oil and a generous amount of pepper, and pour over the salad. Serve immediately.

235 Calories per serving

NOT SUITABLE FOR FREEZING

Pasta Salad with Basil and Cheese

Serves 4

175 g (6 oz) dried tricoloured pasta twists
salt and pepper
75 g (3 oz) mangetout, trimmed
6 cauliflower florets, very finely sliced
3 spring onions, trimmed and sliced
a small handful of fresh basil leaves
15 ml (1 level tbsp) chopped fresh parsley
75 g (3 oz) Parmesan cheese, cut into small cubes
75 ml (5 tbsp) low-fat French dressing
fresh basil leaves, to garnish

1 Cook the pasta in a large saucepan of boiling salted water for 10–12 minutes or until just tender. Drain and cool under cold running water.

2 Steam the mangetout for 3 minutes, then cool under cold water. Slice very finely diagonally.

3 Mix the vegetables with the pasta, and fold in the herbs and cheese. Stir in the dressing.

4 Cover the salad tightly and leave to stand in a cool place (not the refrigerator) for a minimum of 5 hours and a maximum of 24 hours, stirring it from time to time so that all the flavours mingle thoroughly. Serve garnished with basil leaves.

VARIATION

If you like a strongly flavoured dressing, add a clove of garlic to the French dressing.

COOK'S TIP

This vegetable and pasta salad is perfect for meals in the garden, as well as for picnics – just take some fresh basil leaves wrapped in cling film with you to garnish the salad before serving.

270 Calories per serving

NOT SUITABLE FOR FREEZING

Baby Vegetable and Pasta Salad

Serves 6

350 g (12 oz) dried pasta shapes, such as
shells, bows and twists

salt and pepper

700 g (1½ lb) mixed baby vegetables, such as
courgettes, asparagus tips, sugar snap peas,
patty pan squashes and leeks

60 ml (4 tbsp) olive oil

45 ml (3 tbsp) pesto sauce

125 g (4 oz) black olives, pitted

125 g (4 oz) cherry tomatoes

a handful of mixed salad leaves

a few chopped fresh herbs

1 Cook the pasta in a large saucepan of boiling salted water for 10–12 minutes or until just tender. Drain well.

2 Meanwhile, prepare the mixed baby vegetables, leaving them whole wherever possible. Any larger, slower-cooking vegetables should be halved or quartered. Steam the prepared vegetables until just tender.

3 Whisk together the olive oil and pesto sauce in a small bowl.

4 Put the pasta in a large bowl with the pesto mixture, the steamed vegetables and the olives and tomatoes. Toss well together, taking care not to break up the vegetables.

5 To serve, put the salad leaves in the bottom of a large serving bowl and spoon the pasta mixture over the top. Sprinkle the salad with chopped fresh herbs and serve immediately with fresh crusty bread.

COOK'S TIP

This salad is meant to be served lukewarm rather than hot or cold. However, if you would like to make it in advance and serve it cold, cool the vegetables and pasta completely and refrigerate until required. Let them come to room temperature before spooning them on top of the salad leaves and sprinkling with herbs.

375 Calories per serving

NOT SUITABLE FOR FREEZING

Baby Vegetable and Pasta Salad (above)

Broccoli and Pasta Salad

Serves 4

175 g (6 oz) wholewheat pasta twists
salt and pepper
275 g (10 oz) broccoli florets and chopped stems
15 ml (1 level tbsp) sesame seeds
20 ml (4 tsp) sunflower oil
1 orange, peeled, segmented and chopped,
with any juice reserved

1 Put the pasta in a saucepan half filled with boiling salted water. Bring back to the boil and place the broccoli in a sieve over the pan. Cover and cook for about 10 minutes or until the pasta and broccoli are tender. Drain and place in a large dish or bowl.

2 Place the sesame seeds in an ungreased heavy-based frying pan and cook over a low heat for 2–3 minutes or until the seeds are just beginning to jump. Crush the seeds in a pestle and mortar, grind them in a coffee grinder or use the end of a rolling pin and a strong bowl.

3 Mix the sesame seeds, oil, orange pieces and any orange juice in a serving bowl. Add the broccoli and pasta, season and toss gently. Cover and chill before serving.

250 Calories per serving

NOT SUITABLE FOR FREEZING

Chicken and Ham Pasta Salad

Serves 8

225 g (8 oz) dried pasta bows
salt and pepper
225 g (8 oz) mangetout, trimmed
400 g (14 oz) can of pitted black olives
125 g (4 oz) smoked cooked ham
450 g (1 lb) cooked chicken breast fillet
150 ml (5 fl oz) natural yogurt
45 ml (3 tbsp) French dressing

1 Cook the pasta in boiling salted water for 10–12 minutes or until just tender, adding the mangetout for the last 2 minutes of cooking time. Drain and cool under cold running water.

2 Halve the olives. Slice the ham and chicken, discarding any fat or skin. Mix with the pasta and mangetout.

3 Mix the yogurt and dressing. Toss the salad in it to coat. Season and serve at once.

300 Calories per serving

NOT SUITABLE FOR FREEZING

*P*ASTA SALAD WITH CHICKEN AND PESTO

SERVES 4

175 g (6 oz) dried mixed tricolour twists and egg pasta spirals

salt and pepper

15 ml (1 tbsp) olive oil

15 ml (1 tbsp) pesto sauce

1 garlic clove, skinned and crushed

6 salad onions, trimmed and sliced

1 bulb of fennel, sliced

125 g (4 oz) cooked cured ham, cut into strips

175 g (6 oz) cherry tomatoes, halved

8 pitted black olives, halved

30 ml (2 level tbsp) chopped fresh mixed herbs

1 Cook the pasta in boiling salted water for 10–12 minutes or until just tender.

2 Meanwhile, gently heat the oil, pesto sauce and garlic in a small pan.

3 Drain the pasta, place in a mixing bowl, pour over the pesto mixture and toss. Cool.

4 Add the salad onions, fennel, chicken, ham, tomatoes and olives to the pasta. Season. Place in a serving bowl and sprinkle with herbs.

265 Calories per serving

NOT SUITABLE FOR FREEZING

INDEX

If you have enjoyed *Good Housekeeping Best Pasta Dishes & Sauces*, you may be interested to know that among a wide range of *Good Housekeeping* publications the following books are also available:

Good Housekeeping Best Dinner Parties (£10.99)

Good Housekeeping Best Summer Food & Barbecues (£10.99)

Good Housekeeping Best 30-Minute Recipes (£10.99)

Good Housekeeping Cookery Club Pasta (£4.99)

These can be found in all good bookshops or call the credit card hotline on 0279 427203
(postage and packing are free).